THE COMEBACK:

Turning Your Life Around With Les Brown

TABLE OF CONTENTS

The Comeback:
Turning your life around with Les Brown

The movie "The Comeback Kid" is emblematic of what it means to triumph after tragedy. The plot of the movie is about Bubba Newman, a rusty minor league baseball player who quit the sport after being disillusioned. Feeling down and out, he decides to coach a group of underprivileged kids. This renews his outlook on life. But following the tragic death of one of the youngsters, the community is united and there is a happy ending.

Life hasn't always been easy. As a child I struggled to find my path and had to fight to get the chances I made for myself. Persistence paid off as, after every put-down, knock-down or rejection, I stuck by my belief, "If you fall, fall on your back…

So that's what I always did, looked up, got up and kept on trying.

My speaking career has inspired many, many others to do the same - turn around their lives.

When I get to hear success stories from those who have turned around their lives - from accidents, poverty, bad luck, self-doubt, whatever hardships they found themselves subjected to - I feel immensely moved and proud. Their resilience and determination helped them come back - because they looked up!

Now I am privileged to be able to share a selection of their stories in this wonderful collaboration of 15 such individuals who have turned their lives around.

These "comeback stories" are personal and inspiring; I hope you too find their determination lights something deep within you all.

Les Brown

A Message From Les

The movie "The Comeback Kid" is emblematic of what it means to triumph after tragedy. The plot of the movie is about Bubba Newman, a rusty minor league baseball player who quit the sport after being disillusioned. Feeling down and out, he decides to coach a group of underprivileged kids. This renews his outlook on life. But following the tragic death of one of the youngsters, the community is united and there is a happy ending.

While this is a movie, it demonstrates the power in comebacks. We all have rough patches in life, but they do not define us and certainly do not become the bookend to our life's story. The title of the movie borrows from the true meaning of what it is to be a comeback kid. It is a person who repeatedly demonstrates the ability to overcome tragedies, and bounce back to triumph and victory. I have often said, if you fall, try and land on your back. Because if you can look up you can get back up. You have what it takes to be a comeback kid. That is comeback power!!! The fact is, "shoot for the moon and even if you miss, you will land amongst the stars." And as far as I am concerned, that is not a bad place to land.

"Life is like a box of chocolates, you never know what you are going to get." Said Forrest Gump. Most assuredly, life is bound to throw you curveballs. How you swing depends on you and the tools you have in your arsenal. And even if you miss, will you quit before you strike out? Or will you get yourself together, adjust yourself and take another nice swing at it. You just might hit a homerun. Stuff will happen and if you are around long enough you will have setbacks. The question is, will you get back up when life knocks you down? You are endowed with the power and resources to achieve more than you can begin to imagine. This is your birthright. You are born to win. But like any game, there are rules to play by. No matter what comes your way, you have the wherewithal to rise above it. You have the superpower to overcome any setbacks. I know this because you have greatness within you. You are indeed a masterpiece, because you are a piece of the Master!!!

The power to succeed at anything lies within each and every one of us. It is our God given birthright to achieve and to succeed. The only limitations that exist are the artificial ones we consciously or subconsciously place on ourselves. Most people like I once was, have bought into negative belief systems and they have successfully talked themselves out of their goals and dreams. For over five decades I have been speaking about the greatness we all possess within. That is, we all have the potential to be great at whatever it is we desire to achieve. In other words, each and every one of us has that special ingredient embedded in our DNA to be great! Most people, however, do not realize this innate power of greatness they have within. It has either been beaten out of them based on their environments or circumstances, or they were never introduced to this unlimited power of greatness they possess within. For some, even if you tell them they possess such unlimited power of greatness it falls flat. It fails to resonate with them. This is because that power within has been weakened and rendered dead by the kryptonite of negative self-talk and belief.

The catalyst that arouses this greatness within is the insatiable hunger to be great. Over the last five decades I have relentlessly said: "You have greatness within, but you've got to be hungry." This has been my mantra. The hunger that I am referring to is what I call the "Magnificent Hunger." That is the hunger that refuses to be satisfied with little teasers. It is the hunger that keeps you up late at night obsessing about your goals and dreams. The hunger pains are relentless and just keep tormenting you until you feed them solutions, finding pathways to achieve your goals and dreams. And when you achieve a particular goal and dream, you set new ones to pursue because the greatness within you is not a one-and-done fluke. It is an endless power source that keeps propelling you to new heights of achievements.

Like most people, I yielded to the negative voices that told me all I could be was mediocre. I was written off and relegated to the eternal abyss of underachiever status. As I have often intimated, my twin brother and I were born on a linoleum floor in an abandoned building in Miami, Florida. Our biological mother had to come to Miami, Florida from Gainesville, GA, (a fact we only recently discovered) to give birth to my brother, Wesley, and I, because she was married and had conceived us out of wedlock. After five weeks of searching for someone willing to take both of us, she found Mrs. Mamie Brown—a woman with no children of her own. The agreement to take us in was conditioned on the fact that she would not separate my brother and I under any circumstances. My biological mother still wanted us to be raised together irrespective of her indiscretion. This turned out to be one the most rewarding things she could have done. I hate to think of what my life would be like if I did not have my twin brother in my life. In this regard, I am grateful. Unfortunately, some twins have been separated at birth or shortly thereafter without knowing that they are twins; in some cases, even if they do know they are a twin, they spend a lifetime looking for their "other half", their sibling.

At school I was a truant, a class clown and I acted those roles out. While my twin brother, Wesley was a standout model student, I often came home with reports from school that earned me Mrs. Mamie's switch. This truancy ultimately got me the unenviable mislabeling of being "educable mentally retarded," ("EMR"). As a result, I was put back in grades twice to repeat classes and then placed in "special education." Let me tell you something; there is nothing special about special ed. It is actually a euphemism. Anyway, after several bouts with medical challenges, one of which threatened my ability to speak, I overcame the odds. I became the Les Brown the world knows today. All the setbacks that I have had to endure in my life only fortified my resolve to succeed and make something out of my life. More importantly, they strengthened my desire to help people move from setbacks to comebacks; from being victims to being victors. And from stepping out of their mental conditioning and mislabels to writing chapters in their life's book. Only this time, it is a book of greatness starring you as the author.

Conventional wisdom had me destined for abject failure. I was supposed to be one of those statistical failures relegated to being consumed by the neighborhood thuggery, druggie and criminality. But fate had a different narrative for my life. I am living proof that what others may think of you does not have to be your story. Being mislabeled EMR did nothing to boost my confidence or grades. Instead, I opted to wear that title proudly. I went on to act out even worse after that. If I was going to be labeled that, I might as well be the best at it. After all, there was no incentive or pressure to do good or earn decent grades. If I am mislabeled as being a "distinguished" member of the "dodo" ward, why not be one, right? So, I became that. I even earned the decorative moniker of "DT" – "The Dumb Twin," by the class. As we all know, some children can be brutal. My classmates were no exception. Well, my twin brother Wesley was considered the smart one while you guessed it, I was the beneficiary of the antithesis. But all these unfortunate events will come to an abrupt halt with the divinely orchestrated interruption of Mr. Leroy Washington, the school's speech and drama teacher.

Fate intervened by way of me going to look for my close friend, McArthur Stevens, who happened to be in Mr. Washington's class. You see, when things are destined to happen, all the stars and pieces align to bring it about. Because I was part of the special ed class, it didn't really matter if I attended my class or not. So, I was free to loiter and wander aimlessly. This day my adventuring took me to Mr. Washington's class. Not only was Mr. Washington a celebrated teacher, but he was also a mentor to young pupils. Seeing that I was loitering, and not one to pass up on an opportunity to mentor an errant kid, he invited me to come solve a problem he had on the blackboard. With my head held down, I told him I could not. I did not even bother to look up at the board to ascertain if I could solve it or not. I automatically resorted to my default safe place of being "Mr. Dodo the DT."

He asked why I could not solve the problem, but before I could answer the class erupted in laughter. So, Mr. Washington asked the class why they thought this was amusing. To what seemed like a choral line, the class shouted, "he's DT." With a puzzled expression he asked, "what is the meaning of DT?" My head still hanging down, I answered, "dumb twin....I'm ....I'm the dumb twin sir." To which the class shouted, "he's the dumb twin." "His twin brother Wesley is smart." Like a rocket shooting into orbit Mr. Washington darted to where I was standing. He grabbed my shoulders, spun me around and grabbed my teary face to look into his eyes. With a stern look he barked, "look at me young man!!!" As stern as his words were, there was genuine love and empathy in his voice. I felt him at that moment, and he had all my attention. He went on to say, "young man, someone else's opinion of you does not have to become your reality." "Do you hear me?" With those simple but potent words, Mr. Washington forever changed my life. I have shared this story so many times but each time it has a different resonance with me.

I began to shadow Mr. Washington. I became a staple fixture in his classes. He literally lit a fire in me, and he put feather to wings. As time went by my belief in myself was slowly restored and I found a renewed purpose to excel. All because of the words of Mr. Washington. He saw the genius in me when others saw me as EMR, the dodo man and DT. Because of his belief in me and his fondness for oration, I started memorizing Webster's dictionary. I went from DT to "Mr. Websters" and "Mr. Vocabulary." One thing was certain, I misused and slaughtered most of the words, and basically had Mr. George Merriam, the co-author of Merriam-Webster's dictionary, turning in his grave by my misuse of his name and words. But I felt great. I felt like somebody again. All it took was for someone to believe in me. Sometimes, you have to rely on someone else's belief in you until your own belief kicks in.

My hunger for greatness became insatiable. I went on to graduate high school, and with Mr. Washington's continued influence and mentoring, I landed an unglamorous job at a local radio station in Miami, Florida. Landing this job came with its own drama, but it became my launchpad for my resilience, determination and stubborn resolve to make something special of myself. Mr. Washington told me I had greatness in me, and I believed him! As I often retell:

"A setback is a setup for a comeback!!!"! So says my good friend and mentee, Dr. Willie Jollie. I have always subscribed to the notion that obstacles are nothing but ladders to success, and the highway to success is always under construction. Life is an evolving series of events, and not a constant or fixed destination. So, there will always be peaks and valleys, ups and downs, and in-between. This is what I refer to as the seesaws of life. You have the power to rise above whatever setbacks you encounter. Brace yourself and begin to visualize all of your setbacks as life's lessons designed for you to grow.

One dogged trait in all successful people is their resilience and a no-matter-what attitude. They take on a task and commit to excelling at it no matter what.

Notwithstanding the obstacles or setbacks they may encounter, (and believe me they encounter so many), they find ways to keep on trucking ahead. Like I have always said, "if you fall try and land on your back." Successful people fall several times over, but they land on their backs and always find ways to get back up. There is no success without trials, tribulations and setbacks. But rather than be discouraged and quit because of setbacks, successful people use those setbacks as energizers to propel them forward. They never, ever give up. Like all successful people, I got my own early education in resilience from Mr. Washington.

With my newly found confidence I decided I wanted to be a radio station disc jockey. A disc joker sounded more like it. The problem was, I had no college education, nor did I have any prior experience working as a disc jockey. I had not even worked at a record store, let alone a radio station. Sometimes, being a little ignorant can strip us of our fears, and instead instill in us confidence that we may not have at all. All I knew was that I wanted to be a radio station disc jockey. So, I hightailed to the local radio station where I met the station manager, a towering stubby guy named Milton "Butterball" Smith. He got the name "Butterball" probably because of his over-imposing, larger than life stature. Let's say he did not shy away from the food table. He was a college football standout at Tennessee State University, where he earned his degree in communication/broadcasting. He was well accomplished and was a pioneering radio personality who rubbed shoulders with celebrities. He was actually one of America's first R&B DJs. He knew radio. So, you can imagine me walking up to him for a job with no education or prior experience.

Here I was, soaking wet toilet paper with nothing more than Mr. Washington's infused-confidence asking for a job as a disc jockey. As soon as he found out I had no college degree or prior radio experience, his bark for me to get lost almost rattled the doors off their hinges. It was enough to send shivers down a crazed dog. I left there and went straight to Mr. Washington, dejected. Rather than dismiss me, he advised me not to take rejections personally. More importantly, he said resilience and persistence always paid off. That was all I needed to hear from my mentor. The next day, bright and early, I was back at the radio station where I saw none other than Mr. Butterball himself. His look told me he was in no mood for my antics.

He asked; "What are you doing here today?"

"I'm here looking for a job." I responded. He shot back saying; "weren't you here yesterday, and didn't I tell you I had no job for you?" with a broad smile, as if I did not notice his contempt for me, I said; "well sir, I was not sure if someone called in sick, quit or got fired" His anger was understandably palpable.

He shot back at me; "Hey, no one quit or got fired, and no one called in sick. Now get out of here." "Yes sir." I answered without a hint of disappointment.

The very next day, with a newly minted smile and confidence as if the previous two days had not occurred, I was back at the same radio station. This time, you could see the steam emanating from Mr. Butterball's nostrils. His anger was not veiled. Shouting and almost foaming from the mouth he snarled; " young man, weren't you here the past two days looking for a job?" "Yes sir!" I answered cheeringly. "Didn't I tell you I had no job for you?" I answered with all the enthusiasm I could muster, "Yes sir, I didn't know if someone died or ..." He was mortified. Before I could finish my sentence, he went berserk. "No one got sick, and no one died. Now get the heck out of here."

The next day guess who was back bright-eyed, with a broader smile than the previous days. Mr. Butterball looked at me in utter shock and disbelief, but deflated as he shook his head, and in a subdued tone said; "go get me some coffee." "Yes Sir" I darted off to get him his coffee. I became the best coffee boy at the radio station. From then, my journey in radio commenced. My resilience, determination and perseverance paid off.

While I did not get my dream job as a radio station disc jockey, I at least had gotten my foot in the door. My opportunity would soon come. As the saying goes, "opportunity sits by patiently waiting for you to recognize and let it in." This I did. While being a goffer at the station I built trust amongst the radio personalities there. I was eager to serve in whatever capacity. And this included running all sorts of errands for them. They even allowed me to use their cars to go pick up guests from the airport though I had no driver's license. When I would deliver food to them in the control room, I would linger around and watch all their moves. I was memorizing all their movements and handling of the console and controls. At times, they would catch on and kick me out. But I was undeterred.

Soon, they all liked me, and they did not mind me hanging around. I was allowed to pick up celebrities like Diana Ross and the Supremes, The Temptations, Sam Cooke, and other famed celebrities of the time. Each day at the station I was biding my time. My time would soon come. One day, one of the disc jockeys named "Rock" could not continue his program. He was wasted, drunk and so inebriated he could barely put together a coherent sentence. This weekend I was the only one at the station so no one could fill in for him. To say I was glad at this development would be an understatement. I paced back and forth watching him through the control room window like a lion stalking prey. All I kept muttering was, "C'mon drink, Rock, drink." I would have gladly supplied him with more if he wanted. I was hungry and ready!!!

It did not take long for the phone to ring with Mr. Klein, the head station manager on the other end of the line.

He said, "Hi Les, Rock can't finish his show."

I smiled even though he couldn't see me and said, "I know sir."

He asked if I could call one of the other disc jockeys to come fill in. I said, "yes sir." And hung up. After I hung up, I did not even consider his request to call anyone to come in and finish Rock's show. I thought to myself, Mr. Klein must think I'm crazy. Instead of calling one of the other disc jockeys, I called my mama and my girlfriend, Cassandra, and told them to turn the radio on because I was about to get on the air. Before they could ask any questions, I hung up. I waited for about 15-minutes, which seemed like an eternity, before calling Mr. Klein back to tell him I could not reach any of the other disc jockeys. In an exasperated voice he asked if I knew how to work the controls.

I said, "yes sir," doing everything I could to hide my utter exhilaration. He followed up saying, "boy, you go in there and finish Rock's show, but don't say anything. Hear me?"

I almost shouted, "Yes sir" in sheer excitement. I hurriedly got in the control room, got Rock out of the chair and took my seat behind the controls like I was a seasoned pro who knew what he was doing. I fired up the controls, activated the microphone, and there began my long career as a radio station disc jockey. I went on to become program director and station manager across different radio markets. I went from a rejected novice to an illustrious coffee boy, and then disc jockey. I was hungry!

When opportunity presented itself, I quickly recognized it, and fearlessly took full advantage of it. What if I had quit when I first encountered Mr. Butterball at the station when I went for the job? What if I had been discouraged after the multiple rejections? Even more, what if I had not recognized my opportunity in Rock's irresponsible behavior? I have often said, "coincidences are God's way of staying anonymous." Mere wanting, wishful thinking and desiring alone are insufficient by themselves to accomplish your goals and dreams. You must have passion and an insatiable hunger for your goals and dreams. You have to make your hunger your motivating force. This will in turn develop and grow in you and activate the sheer resilience and no-quit attitude necessary for success. If not you, who? And if not now, when? Along with this, you must imbue yourself with the strength of purpose to persevere no matter what temporary setbacks may prevail on you. With this, the embers of your hunger flames will become raging fires. You have got to tune out distractions and negative energies. In other words, you have got to saturate yourself with a do-or-die attitude. Oftentimes, fears are the result of lack of focus, stress, lack of goals, lack of dreams and lack of preparation. Therefore, preparation is always instrumental in success.

My thought process has always been "luck is when

preparation meets opportunity." So, I have made it a point all through my 52-year plus career to be and stay prepared. Even the mundane tasks I take on I make sure I prepare for them. I am constantly refining and reinventing myself. All successful people do the same. I remember when I first got into the speaking and coaching business, I used to make at least 100 calls a day using the street corner payphones. Back then there were no cell phones, smartphones, Google, emails, or social media. Home/land phones were a privilege and luxury not too many had. So, the convenient alternative was to go, your coins in hand, to the street payphones. By the way, weather conditions were no barriers. If you could brave the weather conditions, and the obnoxious people either using or waiting to use the phone then you made your calls. So, imagine making a minimum of 100 calls a day. I am quite sure most people today do not even know what the corner street payphones look like. How far we have come from that to smartphones that are basically minicomputers in your palms.

Those days I developed calluses in my ears from making so many phone calls to get speaking engagements and coaching clients. I made it a point to speak to anyone within three feet of me, and at least 15 people daily. My ears were like cauliflower. The same condition wrestlers and fighters can develop. Nothing worth having comes easy. You have to put in the effort. And, you have to believe in yourself while ignoring naysayers.

Somehow, we have been preconditioned to believe that life is a bed of roses and if there is any hint of challenges or setbacks then we are doomed. As a society we define ourselves only by our successes, and condemn those caught in the struggles of achieving their goals and dreams as failures. We have become totally impatient and disconnected from the processes to success themselves, with only an end-result mindset. This is not how success typically works. In fact, there will be more setbacks than successes. Each one of those perceived setbacks or obstacles is indeed an opportunity disguised as such. They are actually indispensable gifts wrapped as problems waiting for us to unwrap them. Once you unwrap them and figure out the enigma, you find yourself much closer to your desired goal. The trouble is, at the first hint of a setback, we throw our hands in the air in despair and give up. There is picture and story that illustrate this point.

During the gold rush out West, there was once this dreamer who had ambitions of striking gold in the fields of California. So, off he went with his family. The prospect of striking it rich with gold had him giddy. So, he purchases all the gear needed and off he goes. Reality soon sets in that this dig for gold was much more than he had bargained for. Along the way he encountered disillusioned people who had failed miserably and some even literally took their lives having spent all their resources to no avail. It did not take long before our friend would realize that he was out of his league and his digging for gold was going to be an exercise in futility. After much pondering and deliberations with his wife and family, he decided to give up and return to the workforce. What he did not know, however, was that he was only a few inches away from striking it filthy rich. His land was actually loaded with premium gold underneath. But he gave up too soon, and caved to the demands of setbacks. Sadly, so many of us are like this gold explorer. We give up when we encounter setbacks. What we may not know is how close we may be to accomplishing our desired goals and dreams. The very next step could be what breaks the dam and outpour. But we quit too soon without allowing the process to actually take hold.

Rock bottom is not always such a bad thing. Is it painful? Of course it is. Can it lead to depressive states and a myriad of maladies? You bet it does. However, if wishes were horses everyone would ride them. Challenges and setbacks reintroduce us to ourselves. It can either fortify our resolve or break us. Take for example, Rabbi Yitzi Hurwitz, of Los Angeles, California, who until recently was a loving husband, devoted father, and Chabad rabbi who enjoyed his community, dancing and playing the guitar. The ALS struck him and completely upended his life. This debilitating condition would essentially re-write his entire life and that of his family. He lost use of his body and extremities. He could no longer hug his wife and children, dance, play the guitar or move his body. He was paralyzed from his neck down. But his condition did not stop him. He found new ways of expression and communication. And his purpose in life was re-invigorated. He refused to be stopped by ALS. The disease had nothing on him. Rabbi Yitzi said, I have a purpose and mission much bigger than myself and ALS. He realized that he had a higher mission and was inspiring people, not as a victim, but as a victor. He learned to write with his eyes. According to him, his love for people will not be diminished and he will find ways to uplift people. He said, "I use my eyes to type heartfelt thoughts for everyone to enjoy."

Even in the face of his own challenges and what may be rightfully described as a season of woes, he found new pathways to enrich others with his uplifting thoughts. Isn't that something? Think about it. Rather than blame God and be angry at the world, or wallow in self-pity, he chose to praise God in spite of, and with, his condition. His eyes have become his pen to communicate with the world. His smiles light up rooms, and his love, kindness, warmth and deep faith are undeniable. Under such circumstances, most people will forego faith, belief, values and even God. But not rabbi Yitzi. He decided to use whatever means to amplify his faith, belief, values and trust in God. His faith and trust in God remain unrelenting and undeterred. He is and should be an inspiration to humanity. Talk about a comeback story. This is a comeback of epic proportion. His enriching columns can be found at torahfrommyeyes.com and on YouTube.

Every setback is really a stepping stone to something much better. All it takes is shifting your perspective from that of setback mentality to a victor mentality. There is no negative circumstance that cannot be turned around. Every challenge has a potential solution hidden within it. It is just a matter of calming down and digging deep into our innate abilities to overcome and transform.

When Jeff Bezos decided to start Amazon, he encountered serious challenges. But he did not quit. After graduating with honors from an ivy league school he landed a succession of plush jobs with some prestigious firms on wall street earning 7 figures.

By any metric he should have been content and settled into the 9-to-5 grind. But he realized that there had to be more. So, he kept on looking. Soon, that opportunity would present itself in the form of an assignment from his boss. He was tasked with monitoring the new internet technology in relation to customer acquisition, engagement and use. At the time the internet was relatively new with a lot of skeptics about its viability and sustainability. Internet then was dial-up and not 5-G, Wi-Fi, and all the new bells and whistles of today. Notwithstanding all the naysayers and skeptics, young Jeff saw a promising trend and a potential worthy of pursuit. Over his boss's vociferous objections and pressure otherwise, Jeff quit his plush job to pursue his passion.

As hard as he tried, he could not convince his boss to come along with him. Each time he was met with a resounding rejection and counsel to go visit a shrink because he was crazy. True, Jeff was indeed crazy. He was just crazy and hungry about his goals and dreams. Undeterred, Jeff left with his new love and co-worker, McKenzie, who believed in him. He had little savings, but a big vision and hunger. With borrowed money from his parents, they hit the road out West. He had done his market research, and to an extent, a study of e-commerce which he was about to launch. He decided his initial product would be books, and since the largest book distributors were in the Seattle area, he thought that was the logical destination. Along the way, he recruited some techies to help with technological integration. Upon reaching Seattle, he started Amazon in his garage and used a door as his office desk. Both he and McKenzie were the order takers, customer service representatives, shippers, and operators of the budding business. They were both hungry to create something much larger than themselves and found a way to do it. Decades later, Amazon is the most valued company in the world. I have often wondered how his old boss, the skeptic who told him to go see a shrink, feels these days after passing up on the opportunity to be a billionaire.

Like Jeff Bezos, in order to succeed, you must become an innovator and an active participant in your life. You must be a risk taker. As David Henry Thoreau eloquently stated; "do not seek a path already blazed. Go where no path exists and leave a trail." Become a trailblazer! You have got to make your obsession your crusade. Whatever your product or dreams are, get them out there massively. Fear has no place on the trail to success. As astutely noted by Zig Ziglar, FEAR as an acronym is, False Evidence Appearing Real. I am encouraging you to activate your faith and Finding Answers In The Heart. You must identify your inhibiting memories in your life, seek help if needed and get past them. To help with this, you must replace all negative memories with positive affirmations and experiences. The limitations you perceive, and the negative things internalized may strictly be the world's view, but that which empowers you and infuses you with your GOD-given abilities and endless possibilities emanates from within your core. You are born with greatness!

External influences and episodes in your life chip away at your greatness if you do not have the right influence and mindset to build you up. "Life is a fight for territory and once you stop fighting for what you want, what you do not want will automatically take over." It is incumbent on you to fight for your goals and dreams. You must open yourself to your individual endless possibilities. Marcus Aurelius, the great Roman Emperor and Stoic once astutely noted that, "the universe is change; our life is what our thoughts make it." So, think positive thoughts, and dare to dream of an opulent life for yourself. My favorite book says, "as a man thinketh in his heart, so is he." James Allen in his classic book, "As a man thinketh," was based on this same idea. All great inventions and innovations began with imaginations and thoughts. Famed scientist, Albert Einstein famously expressed that "imagination is more important than knowledge." He reasoned that, "knowledge is limited, whereas imagination embraces the world, stimulating progress, giving birth to evolution." He went on to say, "imagination is a preview to life's coming attractions." Dream big and then discover ways to achieve your goals and dreams. Be relentless and resilient in your pursuit. Failure is not an option. True failure is actually the inaction!! Michael Jordan once alluded to this when he recalled that you miss 100% of the shots you do not take.

Move! Take Charge! Action!!! Action!! Action! There is the time to think, plan, ruminate and the demand to yield to logic. Most times however, logic, reason and overthinking can get in the way of your progress. Childlike abandon is required to take you to the highway of your dreams. And even if your desired goals and dreams are not initially achieved, persevere and press on ahead. Remember, "in the confrontation between the stream and the rock, the stream always wins, not through strength but by perseverance." That is how H. Jackson Brown observed it.

Another inspiring figure is Stephen Hawking, the English physicist, cosmologist and mathematics professor who went on to accumulate so many distinguished accolades for his achievements and contributions to science. Born in Oxford, England into a family of physicians, he got his standard of achievement early in life. At 17 he enrolled in the university where he would earn a first-class B.Sc degree in physics. He would then go on to earn his PhD in applied mathematics and theoretical physics with an emphasis in general relativity and cosmology. However, tragedy would soon strike young Stephen. At 21 years old, he got diagnosed with a debilitating form of motor neurone disease, ALS. This disease would eventually paralyze him and rob him of his ability to speak. Can you imagine being a professor and not being able to speak to your students? Incredible, indeed. Notwithstanding, he remained resilient, and he refused to be defined or cabined to his condition. He would not allow his mind and contributions to lay idle or go to waste in the winds of despair. So, he resorted to communicating with speech-generating devices through use of a handheld switch.

When use of his hands became a challenge, he remained unstoppable. By using a single cheek muscle, he was still able to activate the speech-generating device so he could continue communicating. This is what resilient people do. They refuse to be stopped. They find ways to forge ahead no matter what. They have the resilience and fortitude of titanium. Their willpower and determination to succeed at all costs, and by any means necessary, should be an inspiration to all of us and a model to emulate. Many of us have our own experiences and stories to lean on, and we should always recall how we persevered. You cannot have a winner's mindset and have a defeatist's life. They just do not go together. You have to cultivate the mindset to keep getting up and pressing ahead, no matter the obstacles, or, for that matter, how many times you fall.

In order to accomplish your goals and dreams, you must have a clearly defined and refined vision. This will be your roadmap to your destined goals and dreams, and it will serve to ignite your hunger. This will ultimately unleash your Greatness!!!! A very important tool to use is: **S.M.A.R.T.**

S=Specific – your goal must be specific enough.

M=Measurable—Your goals must be measurable in terms of how long it should take.

A=Achievable—It does not help to set goals that are clearly not attainable. Know yourself.

R=Relevant—You have to ensure your goals are not absurd and purposeless.

T=Time-bound—The goals are timed for execution.

THE POWER OF VISION

Vision opens the portal to your goals and dreams in ways that cannot be overstated. Without vision your goals and dreams are like a ship without a rudder. Imagine traveling from New York to California without GPS or a map. What are your chances of getting to your destination? Now imagine for a second that you had a very important meeting there to close a very lucrative deal that will net you a financial windfall. And you had to get there at a specified time otherwise the deal would be off. So, you get in your car because that is your only mode of transportation to get you there. But then you realize you have no Waze or Google maps because such technology was not available. You also realize you do not have a map, compass or navigational device. Well, you get the picture. How will you get to California to close your deal? You might just find yourself in Mexico, Canada or heading straight into the ocean.

Similarly, without a vision you are headed nowhere. It is a recipe for purposeless living and unfulfilled life. Vision is pertinent to both your personal and professional lives. How do you see yourself in the future? What kind of life, family, health and relationships do you envision having? And with regards to your career or business, what are the outlooks for the future? What are the short- and long-term projections? Vision has power in shaping how you plan. Vision gives you a sense of direction and helps you with decision-making. Vision motivates you and everyone aligned with you. More importantly, vision challenges you. Having positive visions of the future for your goals and dreams is essential to your success.

Your vision is your lifeline because it is intricately linked to your thoughts. Your vision emanates from your thoughts and perceived notions. You typically craft your vision from your thinking and ideas. Therefore, positive vision for your future is the most powerful and forceful motivation for attaining your goals and dreams. The belief that visions are elusive or unattainable should be outrightly dispelled. Nothing could be further from the truth.

The power of your vision directs your path and illuminates your future. It clarifies, it answers questions, and it brings understanding and purpose. It undergirds your driving force within you and awakens what may be a dormant greatness already within you. It propels and anchors you, and it becomes your attracting passion that inspires and motivates you. Your positive vision of where you would like to be in the future is what animates you. If I were to ask you right now to succinctly and concisely describe what your life would look like in the next five years can you articulate it with enough clarity? Where would your relationships, family and professional outlook be in five years? Are you living a fulfilling and rewarding life at the moment? Is this all life has for you? Life asks of us to step outside the ordinary and our comfort zones in order to be extraordinary. Those who do enjoy remarkable successes. You are born a winner. You are not an accident.

You want to talk about someone being unstoppable?

Alonzo Herndon is your prototype. As a former slave and sharecropper born to his white enslaver and enslaved woman named Sophenie, Alonzo had every marking of an abject failure. His father never accepted paternity. They were relegated to severe poverty and an abysmal living on the farm as slaves. After the civil war, his "father" sent him and his mom away penniless into homelessness and extreme poverty. So, to help with their subsistence, young Alonzo became a laborer and peddler of peanuts, homemade molasses and axle grease. As a young man his entrepreneurial ambition was evident. With his meager earnings he was able to set aside a small portion toward his goal of entrepreneurship. All along he had his mind set on leaving his harsh life at Social Circle, Georgia as soon as possible, and he knew he would need resources to bring that about. Depending on an outside savior was not an option for him. He realized that it would be up to him to take the mantle of his future in his own hands.

He was determined even at a young age to improve his and his family's economic and social conditions. He did not know how, but he refused to accept the life they lived as his fate and destiny. He had a vision of a better future and life. The details and in-betweens would have to come later. He followed the blueprint of successful people even with just one year of education in his entire life. That is, he had the thought of a better life, but he had no resources. He was hungry. The thought was transferred into his vision. His relentless hunger morphed from vision into action. Eventually, at twenty years old, he left his family at Social Circle, GA, walking on foot with just eleven dollars to his name. Along the way he worked as a farmhand and decided that his ticket out of poverty was to learn barbering. Subsequent to which he traveled to Jonesboro, Georgia, to begin a barbering career. Rather than settle, he decided to partner with the owner of one of the barbershops he worked at. This effectively made him a co-owner after so many years of paying his dues and saving his money. He would go on to open three more barbershops of his own. One of which would be considered the premier barbershop in Atlanta, and the entire South.

"The Crystal Palace Barbershop" became the spot where the most powerful, influential and elite Atlantans went to get groomed. His barbers were all Blacks and the most skilled. And he personally supervised the grooming of his clients to ensure that they had an experience and left satisfied. Which they did. Ironically, and rather unfortunately, because of the atmosphere of the period, none of his barbers were allowed to get a haircut at the shop. Not even Alonzo, the owner himself. This did not stop Alonzo. He dug his head down and remained committed to his dreams. Even when the Atlanta race riot resulted in the destruction of his shop, he reopened bigger and better while being glad to be alive. Black shop owners across the street to his barbershop were dragged out and killed on the street. Fortunately for him, he had gone home early.

He persevered and went on to own over 100 real estate properties, a large block of commercial real estate, schools, and Atlanta Life Insurance Company, which expanded to six states. The insurance company is still operational today, long after his death in 1927. At the time of his passing, he was considered one of the wealthiest Black men in America. The story of Alonzo's journey, from slavery to being a multimillionaire entrepreneur, typifies and embodies hunger and someone who was determined to win against all odds. He was able to overcome several setbacks to create a life and legacy that is outliving him. That is the spirit of winners. They refuse to settle for a mediocre life. There is something about setbacks that propel them forward. They just keep plugging and finding ways to get things done.

No matter what circumstances surround your birth you should know that you already beat the odds to be here. You actually fought hard for your existence. You are the only one who survived from the millions of potentials to become the you that you see in the mirror every day. Do not take this for granted. But to enjoy your prize for being born you must get in the game of life to win. You must look past your current reality and dare to visualize the wonderful possibilities that lay ahead. Allow yourself to imagine and visualize. No need to be afraid. Give yourself permission to bring your imagination to life. It's yours and solely yours. Yes, YOU!! And the world is anxiously waiting. That is the power of vision.

Alonzo had a vision of an opulent future diametrically opposed to his slavery days. He desired more out of life, and he visualized himself a successful businessman. That's vision power.

The ingredient to succeed is a clear vision and the unrelenting hunger to achieve your goals and dreams. You have to be unapologetically focused and determined. It is your life. If your life is focused and purposeful you will find joy, happiness, reward and fulfillment. With a lucid vision you can transform your life from mediocre and ordinary to exceptional and extraordinary.

Vision boards have become a staple these days. But most people crowd their vision boards based on the belief that the aesthetics of the board is better than substance. This is not necessarily the case. To help with your vision here are a few tips:

- Your vision should state your short- and long-term goals with clarity and detail. Your short-term goals help you get to your long-term goals.
- Your vision should reflect your personal values and beliefs. Honesty, creativity, loyalty and all pertinent information should be in it.
- Your vision should show your interests. What are

you passionate about?

- Your skill sets, strength and traits should be in your vision.
- Your areas of need, weakness and improvement.
- What difference do you hope to make?
- Use the vision board to illustrate your vision.

With your vision clearly defined, you can now start to take some action steps. Remember, there are no failures in moving toward your goals and dreams. The only failures are goals not attempted. So, step out of the shackles of your mind and begin the journey to your new YOU!

EMBRACE FAILURE

Failure can and should be your learning tool. "Life be lifeing." My favorite book says, "think it not strange that you will face the fiery trial," you will (--not you might), surely face your fair share of challenges. If you live long enough you will certainly face your individually wrapped ups and downs designed just for you. Life is all about peaks and valleys. Each one of those moments presents you with unique experiences disguised as challenges. A shift in mindset is the key to overcoming these temporary setbacks. You should condition your mind to begin to see those challenging moments as Blessings disguised as trials. They are gifts designed to elevate you to newer heights... in essence they are opportunities wrapped in the packages of challenges. What do you do with wrappers of candies or gifts? You discard them. So, discard those worries that tend to rob you of your greatness.

Sometimes, if not most, people focus more on the problems rather than the solutions staring right at them. Unfortunately, the more you focus on the problems, the larger they become until they overwhelm you. On the flip side of that coin, the problems become smaller and obscured when a solutions mindset is activated. One important question to always ponder is, of eight billion people on earth, why did this trial choose you? Think about it. Why?

Apparently, there is something in you that is tailor-made to handle the challenge. Just like your birth was not an accident, so it is that the trial is not. You have the wherewithal to handle whatever challenges come your way. Without you the world would not be complete. You were born for a reason with a specific mission, a specific contribution, and the tools to succeed. If you do not accede to it, your mission will be left undone, and the world will be deprived of your specific contribution. Without your contribution it will be like driving a car without wheels. Or like riding a bike with one wheel. I am not talking about a unicycle either. I am talking about a two-wheel bicycle missing one wheel. That is how important you are to the world.

Most people look at failures as a wholesome devastating event. To them, one failure begets another failure, and so continues the vicious cycle. Until, of course, they find themselves in an abyss. Nothing, however, could be further from the truth. Each failure is actually an eliminating process so you can focus on the next option. Thomas Edison went through over 20,000 failed experiments to finally solve his challenge of inventing the light bulb. The way he saw it was that they were not failures or setbacks, instead they were 20,000 ways he discovered that his discovery would not work. In fact, there is no innovation, invention or discovery that did not have a plethora of failures. The great Michael Jordan missed 12,345 shots out of 24,537 career field goals. He actually missed more than he made. Yet he is regarded as the greatest basketball player ever. His missed shots cannot be considered failures because he actually gave himself the chance for them to go in by shooting the balls. There was a fifty-fifty chance that he either might make or miss them. You just never know when victory and vindication will come.

Failures are woven into the fabric of our lives, plain and simple. We cannot escape this. Yet, it is essential to our learning and growth. Do not use failures as a dead end. Failure should be your learning tool and guide. Here are some benefits of failures:

- Understand that failures are part of the process to discovery and move on. Do not dwell on them.
- Have no fear of failures. Embrace them and pause before rushing to judgment. Celebrate the process and pivot to a new way. All failures present learning opportunities, so take full advantage of them. Take risks anyways.
- Learning is an ongoing process and not a zero-sum game. Mis[takes] are part of the process as well. It is not your first time to err, nor will it be your last. Make mis[takes] anyways.
- Failure is your springboard and motivator. Use it. Make it serve you and not enslave you. Yes, failures do take emotional tolls and it may be difficult to pick the pieces and move on. But do it anyways. What is the alternative? Is it to curl in a fetal position all day to sulk until you disintegrate into air? A child falls several times and sometimes hits their head as they learn to walk. But they continue to try. Just like riding a bike, you are bound to fall while learning to ride, but you ride anyway.
- Do not run away from failures. Instead, weave its possibilities in everything you do. Expect it. Anticipate it and look out for it. Be prepared ahead for it.

- Do not keep it to yourself. Share your experiences with trusted people in your circle.
- Remember! There is no such thing as perfection. So, practice does not make perfect. Dismantle that nonsensical belief system. Instead, practice makes better!!

As Micheal Jordan eloquently put it, "pressure is nothing more than the shadow of great opportunity." And my dear friend Stephen Covey added that, "effective people are not problem-minded, they're opportunity-minded. They feed opportunities and starve problems. In other words, "new beginnings are often disguised as painful endings." So said Lao Tzu. And, as per Ralph Waldo Emerson, "every wall is a door." Find opportunities in problems. Therein lies victory. You are a victor not a victim. You are born to win because you are a hot-wired winner. But you must engage in life's game to win. Give yourself a chance at victory and cultivate a resilient mindset. This is your mission statement. Know that being a failure is not your portion. It is not your destiny, nor is it your fate!! Win! That is your call to action.

DEVELOPING A RESILIENT MINDSET

We are all innately resilient in some regard. But there are those who are obvious and highly resilient. We know stories of people's formidable achievements, and we often wonder, how did they do that? Or how did they get out of that? The mind is stronger than we credit it for. The ways to develop your resiliency are:

- Know yourself and your capabilities.
- Know the resources you have.
- Find ways to deal with your stress. And avoid negative, toxic people and situations.
- Eat healthy, get enough sleep, stay fit and engage in wellness of the body and soul.
- Be mindful of your surroundings.
- Take full control of your thoughts and feelings. Never give anyone the power of you. Take stock of yourself frequently and do not be afraid to hold yourself accountable.
- Be and stay positive. Avoid negative thoughts and energies. Listen to motivational and meditation music. Even tones and frequencies can be both healing and relaxing.
- Life is full of contradictions. Accept the fact and move on. Change what you can reasonably change, and what you cannot change, move on from. It may just not be the right time.
- Take advantage of your support systems. Study other resilient people.
- Develop effective communicative skills.
- Refrain from the blame game. Be reflective and introspective, and not self-centered.
- Do not fret or be afraid to let go of deadweights.

- Build a community of greatness.

These principles will fortify your resolve and resilience and will save you a lot of heartache. The "rubber band" principle, which holds that it is most effective when stretched because it can hold more things together, should be your life's model. Life's pressures are designed to stretch your resilience and not snap you. That is when you should be at your best. You should stretch yourself to new heights and new potentials during these moments of trial. The "rubber band principle" is helpful with your exercise regimen, dieting and outlook in life. But remember that, like anything in life, if you stretch it too much it will snap. That is the deleterious effects of overloading. So, know your limits. Otherwise, snap goes your rubber band.

Resilience is not survivalist mentality. It is mental toughness. This is enshrined in the four pillars of mental toughness inculcated by the Navy Seals.

1. Goal Setting
2. Mental visualization
3. Positive self-talk
4. Arousal control

As I alluded to before, a setback is your precursor to your comeback. You have comeback power!!! You have greatness within you, but you have to be hungry!!! That is my story, and I am sticking to it. This has been Mrs. Mamie Brown's baby boy, and Dorothy Bell Rucker's pride and joy. Bye for now!!!

DR. SHAMEKA WALKER

An Unafraid Literary Star and Champion for Social Justice, Dr. Shameka Walker embarked on a creative journey, emerging as a renowned and extraordinary writer. The release of her first book, "Love without Fear," in 2013, was a meteoric start to her literary career. Working alongside her spouse, Dr. Samuel Walker, Shameka approaches problems analytically, with the goal of strengthening the principles that are the foundation of relationships. She received an honorary degree from Initiator Christian University in acknowledgment of her community service and life achievement. Shameka finds comfort and happiness in spending time with loved ones when she is not flying the friendly skies as a Flight Attendant. She values the ties that connect her to her heritage, which are strengthened by her large family of siblings. Shameka Walker exemplifies the core principles of integrity and selflessness in everything that she does, with a passion for improving society as a whole. Her life story is one of religion, family, literature, and service.

Chapter 1
"Prayer, Planning & Forgiveness"

DrShameka Walker

askshameka

www.askshameka.com

Prayer, Planning & Forgiveness

Dr. Shameka Walker

Best-Selling Author, Podcaster and Motivational Speaker

Everyone has wins and losses in their lives, successes and failures, and I am no exception. My life has not been perfect, but I've been able to navigate through all the trials and tribulations that have come my way. I am living proof that what truly matters is how you deal with life's adversities. That's the only thing that counts in the end.

Today, I live a full life, playing many roles. I am a wife and mother, daughter, sister and friend to many. I'm a best-selling author, and my husband and I host a YouTube podcast called, "Pillow Talk with the Dr. Walker Duo". I blog and write poetry and short stories about real life issues and situations. My credo is to "love unconditionally, live life to the fullest and enjoy the freedom to be unapologetically happy!"

I was raised in a small rural Mississippi town called Quitman. We had a big family. I was the eleventh born of twelve and the youngest girl. My two heroes growing up were my parents. They taught us to be nice and kind to other people. Even though my parents lost two of my siblings at birth, they were still left with ten kids to feed and look after. Their entire lives were focused on family and raising children. They sacrificed everything to work hard to ensure that we were provided with everything we needed. They made living look easy, even though I realize now, as an adult, that their lives were difficult in many respects.

The only hero or role model outside of my family and small community was Oprah Winfrey from the Oprah Winfrey Show. We owned a TV but could only get a couple of channels by using the antenna. The Oprah Winfrey Show became a source of encouragement, especially after hearing her own personal story. Her positive attitude and willingness to overcome her past challenges fueled my motivation to work harder to achieve a better life than what my past had dealt me. My father was the pastor of the local church, so our parents took us all to church and introduced us to Christianity. I leaned on God for support a lot when I was growing up. I needed support from somewhere because I grew up hiding a dark secret from everyone.

For ten years of my early life, from age four to age fourteen, I was sexually molested. This was not a single incident but ten years full of incidents. I never told my parents or any of my siblings about the abuse because I was confused about it. As a child, I didn't understand who was responsible and who was at fault. I was afraid that if I talked about it, I might get into a lot of trouble. So, because of the sexual abuse, I have an entirely different perspective on my childhood than most people do.

By the time I became a teenager, I understood better that my abusers were at fault and I put a stop to it. I understood that none of it was my fault. At the age of fourteen, when I started high school, I understood that if I didn't speak up, that the abuse was going to continue. That's when everything ended. I told my abusers, "You know, this is not supposed to be happening. This is no longer going to happen. You're not going to put your hands on me anymore! You can't do this to me anymore. This is wrong". God built me in a way that I can withstand difficulties. I prayed to him that if he would allow this to end, then I'd be okay.

I was old enough by that time to handle it on my own. I didn't involve any other adults in the situation at the time. I probably should have, but I didn't feel safe. I didn't feel comfortable talking about it. My parents were not to blame because they had so much to deal with already, with ten children to feed and look after.

I never felt the need for revenge, to retaliate against these people. For that reason, there was no need to discuss it with anyone. "You hurt me, but that doesn't mean that I have to hurt you". No one needed to go to jail. Even though I had a bad experience with them, now they have the opportunity to be somebody else's hero. If they were in jail, then those young people would be denied the positive experience that I had with my parents. I made a conscious decision that as long as I was okay now, then I was okay. Forgive and forget. I decided to stay positive. I prayed and told the

3

Lord that I was determined to find something positive out of all of it. So that's what I did. I didn't want to be someone who moved through life always feeling that hurt, never letting go, always being reminded of it.

I think that decision was as much a benefit for me as it was for them and I've never regretted it. It did not break me, but instead, it made me into the strong person that I am today. I thought that the things I went through as a child, especially since it was with people who were close to our family, I was going to have to see them again. If I didn't move on, I'd be stuck in that mode. Forgiveness isn't just for them, it's also for you. Forgiving set me free from a lot of pain and things that I was holding onto in my heart. I liked the way I felt after I forgave. It lifted a burden off of me that made it so much easier for me to navigate through life. It also set them free, knowing that the damage they had done to me would not stop me from moving on and having a beautiful life.

So now, everyone involved is forgiven and able to move on and live their life. I wanted to see those individuals who hurt me live a purposeful life. And now, they're somebody's hero. They have kids, they've got grandkids and in-laws. There are so many people involved in the big picture by this time. I couldn't let my story be the reason that all of their lives were affected. I chose to carry the burden alone and it's worked out. I'm okay. I truly believe that our pains are necessary in life and it's up to us whether we let our pains break us or make us. I've chosen to allow mine to make me.

Teenage years and beyond

As I got older, I began thinking about becoming a lawyer. I thought it would be good to become an advocate for other people who had gone through what I went through. I've since learned that a lot of sexual abuse victims turn to drug and alcohol abuse. Some of them also become sexually promiscuous, having a lot of sex partners and then let their lives kind of spiral out of control. I've been able to remain intact, physically, mentally and spiritually, because when God created me, he created a diamond. He placed all this pressure on me and now I'm the hardest, toughest thing in the whole universe. That's why I thought I would be good at helping others who were not as strong, who weren't built like me. I could tell them that no matter what their situation is, that with God as their guide, and by trusting in God's plan, they would be okay. God could bring peace into their lives and help them mend all the broken pieces. Throughout my life, I've met many people who experienced the same things I experienced. Since we have that in common, some have become good friends.

When I enrolled in college, I began in the criminal justice program my freshman year with the intent of eventually going to law school. I wanted to help others who had been molested. But I soon switched majors to marketing because I realized what I really wanted to do was to get into business. I'm very happy that I did switch because it put me on the path to where I am today. I've had a very successful career in business.

But even though I never became a lawyer, I still get involved helping other abuse victims. Just because something happened to you in the past, that's not the end of your life. You still have complete control over your present and the opportunity of creating an exciting, energetic future, to be able to live a successful and beautiful life. I have a burning desire to inspire others and motivate them to let them know that life can always be better. Regardless of what life brings your way, you are to learn from those pains, trust God's process, and go out and live a purpose-fulfilled life. Everybody deserves to fulfill their purpose in life.

I've learned that some people have trouble letting go of their past. I try to help them navigate through their pain. It can be a difficult process. Some people get through it faster than others. But the most important thing is, don't stop; don't give up. You have to keep going and allow God to do his thing. He has a plan for us and it's up to us to trust and have faith and do his will instead of our own will. If we follow our own will, it ends up being harder. He won't interfere. He'll let us go ahead until we find out we need him to help guide us. And that's okay. That's part of the process of growth.

This is what I do now, as a first lady, the wife of the pastor at a church in Georgia. I work as a guide, helping people navigate through their pain.

Letting Go and Moving On

I did the work that I needed to do in high school by making good grades, and was very active in sports and other clubs and organizations. This paved the way for me to receive many scholarships so that I could go to the college of my choice. And it wasn't going to be the University of Mississippi or Mississippi State University. I could have easily gotten a full scholarship by remaining in-state. But I had to escape from Mississippi. Even though I had some good memories of growing up in Mississippi, I had too many painful memories in my home state. If I was constantly reminded of what happened, it would be much harder to move forward. My whole life, my future, my mental and emotional wellbeing; it was all at stake. It was time to move on. It was time for a fresh start so that I could begin living the life that I was destined to live. It was imperative that I leave the state of Mississippi.

I applied to Johnson & Wales University in Providence, Rhode Island. New England seemed like it would be far enough away from Mississippi. It turned out to be one of the best decisions of my life. It allowed me to live the life I wanted to live for myself, without being dependent on my parents. I was able to escape all the heartache that I endured as a child, while at the same time, taking all of my good childhood memories along with me. Moving to a new environment helped motivate me to pursue my life's full potential, to eventually become Dr. Shameka Walker. By going to school in Rhode Island, it completely changed my life and allowed me to meet some amazing people.

Some of these people I met in college are now permanent fixtures in my life. Some of my best friends, we all met in college and we're still friends to this day. I wouldn't trade that experience and those friends for anything. Having them in my life has helped make me who I am today. Moving on also put me on a path where I would eventually meet my amazing husband, who I've been married to for twenty-four years. We met in Connecticut after I had graduated from college.

And so, everything was at stake if I wasn't able to learn from my childhood trauma and say, "Okay, I need to put all of this behind me and move on. There's something better for me out here. It's up to me to do the work and go after it." You can't say, "I want better", and then not make any changes. The first thing you need to do is have a change of mindset. That's Imperative. Once you change your mindset, the body is going to follow and then your thoughts will follow.

"When life knocks you down, try to land on your back. Because if you can look up, you can get up."
~Les Brown

If I had stayed back in Mississippi, maybe I would have developed some bad habits. But my mother and father and some of my other friends were big sources of encouragement. They used to say, "If anyone can do it, we know you can do it". They said that, not even knowing about my bad experiences. I didn't tell anyone for many years because I only wanted positive energy in my life.

More Challenges

Experiencing what I experienced as a child and moving on became a source of confidence and inner strength for me. I felt like I could endure whatever challenges and hardships that might come up. When I was in college, I got into a relationship that eventually became abusive. I did well in college. I was an honor student. But getting good grades and having a high level of intelligence doesn't make you immune from attracting some of the wrong people into your life. This was someone I originally saw myself sharing my life with. But those hands that were at first used to embrace me with, were later used to beat me with.

Again, I never told my dad about any of this. I just dealt with it myself. I said to myself, "You got yourself into this so it's up to you to get yourself out of it". Like my childhood situation, I didn't tell anyone about how bad this relationship was because I didn't want anyone else to be burdened with it.

I found myself stuck in a situation that I didn't know exactly how to get out of. I wanted to get out of it, in fact I was determined to get out of it. But while I was in college, I couldn't figure out a way to do it. I was mostly just very cautious, and quite honestly, scared. This man told me in no uncertain terms, right in my face, nose-to-nose, that I would not live another day if I dated another man. And I believed it. So, I stayed in that relationship until I found a way to break free.

After graduation, I got a good job with a good income so that I was financially stable. Then my company gave me a promotion and moved me out of state. Once I had moved, I bounced myself free from that relationship. Because of what had happened to me earlier, I was well-equipped to deal with the situation, even though it took me a while to do it.

It was partly through prayer and just thoughtful planning that I got out of this person's life. By waiting until I could live independently, I ensured myself of a successful outcome. I'm thankful to God that it all worked out. I trusted God and I had that strong relationship with him. He promised to bring me out. It was just that his timing was not the same as my timing, but his timing was definitely on time. I now look at the whole situation as a learning experience.

I left this man for good on a Friday. Two days later, I met the man who would eventually become my husband. He was in the military. We spent a short time together, but he had to leave on assignment for six months. We corresponded and then began dating after he returned.

You have to take all the negatives and find a way to turn them into positives. Negative things are going to happen. It's a process of trial and error, but it's what you do with those situations that determines how quickly and successfully you resolve them. I've had plenty of difficult situations to deal with in my life, and fortunately, I've always found a way to navigate through them. Having the close relationship that I have with God has been a really important factor. Without him, I wouldn't be the child of God that I am and the person that I've become today.

> *"The world is waiting for you to wake up to the person you are called to be."*
> ~ **Les Brown**

So, it was essential for me to make all the changes that I needed to make in order to become the person God wanted me to be. Not who Shameka wanted to be. Shameka wanted a lot of things, but God wanted me to become someone who could be of service to others. He put me here for others, not just for myself. He wanted me to be a beacon of light who could show others how to break free from their past and move on. I'm an advocate for God's children who have become mired in the quicksand of their past experiences. When God sees one of his children stuck in that quicksand, he sends someone with a rope. All you have to do is grab onto the rope and allow yourself to be pulled out. Then once you get yourself out, and you're standing up again on your own, you do the work that needs to be done in order to become a better person and to have a better life. That process begins with changing your mindset.

I've always believed that it's best for me to try to handle everything between myself and God, because if I trust in God, then he's going to help me resolve this. I also realize that there is a bigger picture, a bigger purpose. God gives me challenges in order to strengthen me so that I am better prepared to get through the next challenge. I know now that this is not just important for me to be able to do this, but it's important for everyone.

Partnering With Me

We all have the tendency to make the same mistakes over and over, expecting a different outcome. It's called self-sabotage. That's why it's so important to change our mindset, change our thought process because change is good. People are afraid of change, but change is inevitable. Everything, including us, is in a constant state of change. We just need to make the right changes, the most beneficial changes for the sake of ourselves and our futures.

One of my self-sabotaging tendencies is believing that I can do everything on my own. I've learned, through trial and error, that I can't. Sometimes, when

I thought that God wasn't moving fast enough for me, I decided I could do better on my own. I learned fairly quickly that, no, no; God allows things to happen at his own pace.

I had a tendency to try to make every decision on my own because I wanted to be Miss Independent. "I can do this". I've learned the hard way that sometimes, it's okay to depend on someone else. This is especially true in my relationship with my husband. He wanted an independent woman, and he got that; me. But at the same time, I've seen that many times, I need him for certain things. There are some areas in which he is strong and I'm weak. That's also true, vice versa. Some things I'm stronger in, so we compliment each other. We're a team. Too often I think I can do everything, as long as I have God. Sometimes, God takes the form of a human helper.

"Ask for help. Not because you are weak. But because you want to remain strong."
~ Les Brown

I also can get a little overly confident with my ideas on how things should be done. Maybe headstrong would be a better word. My twenty-three-year-old daughter sometimes says to me, "Mom, you think that if we don't do it your way, then it's just wrong." I've learned over the years to scale back and accept other people's opinions, and also to incorporate the ideas and opinions of others into plans and projects. I've discovered that things often work even better when I don't automatically assume that my way is the best way or the only way. That process didn't happen overnight. I think that stems from not being able to trust and depend on adults in my childhood. I've spent a lifetime proving to myself, and everyone else, that I can do it all on my own.

This was especially true when I was younger, in my twenties. You couldn't tell me anything. I believe in crossing all of my 'Ts' and dotting all of my 'Is'; and doing everything with perfection. I do the research I need to do and check in with all the experts. I strive at doing everything the right way, even better than the experts. My motto is to live a life that you never have to apologize for or make excuses for. Eventually, I came to realize that living like that was very stressful. Then I discovered the idea of teamwork. Delegate and let your team members make the process easier. I'm very thankful that I eventually learned that.

I also have a fear of rejection and a big fear of failure. This is the biggest fear I have in life of not being successful. You can have obstacles and bad things happen to you in life and still be successful. I also used to fear not knowing my life's purpose, or not living up to my life's purpose and potential. God has me here for a reason. Why? Then one day, that revelation came. That is the best feeling anyone can have, knowing what your true purpose is here on earth, as opposed to just living; waking up, going to work, taking care of kids, buying groceries, eating, sleeping, and starting all over the next day. That's not living. Can you be at peace doing that? Absolutely, you can be at peace. You can also be comfortable. But that's not living a purpose-filled life that God wants you to live, that is based on the reason he put you here.

Maybe your reason for being here is just to lead a simple life and work as a bus driver. That's okay, if that's your calling; the reason God put you here on earth. But it is important that everyone figure it out for themselves.

Milestones

I've experienced five major milestones in my life that have created challenges that I've had to overcome, that have ultimately resulted in me growing stronger as a result. The first milestone was my childhood sexual abuse. I bore all of this trauma myself. With my father being the pastor of our local church, at the age of fourteen, I realized that revealing all of it would have created a tornado in our small town.

The second major milestone was the domestic violence I experienced in college and right after graduation. I didn't get my family involved in this situation either, partly because they would have come up and gotten me and taken me back to Mississippi. Returning to Mississippi was not an option.

The third major milestone was meeting my husband and getting married. We dated only six weeks but that's all we needed to know it was right for both of us. One of my husband's biggest dreams was to be a father. The biggest issue I've had to deal with in my marriage is infertility. Again, I had to internalize this. I found the man of my dreams but the fear of possibly never making him a father was overwhelming. It's a very difficult topic to discuss with anyone outside of your own family, especially feelings of inadequacy as a woman. According to my doctor, the infertility stemmed from a combination of polycystic ovarian syndrome (PCOS), my incompetent cervix, and my abuse as a child. It was like a roller coaster; get pregnant, lose the baby, get pregnant, have the baby, get pregnant, lose the baby. The process has created a deep sense of intimacy and compassion between my husband and myself. Fortunately, we're now blessed with three wonderful children.

The fourth milestone in my life was the death of my parents. This has created a closer bond between my siblings. We Zoom together regularly now. We have our disagreements, but we're all old enough and mature enough to work through everything.

My fifth major milestone is my dual career as the first lady of our church and as a flight attendant. Managing my time and juggling responsibilities is a perpetual challenge. Growing up the kid of a preacher didn't make me want to become the first lady of a church. But the job came along with the man of my dreams. I've adapted to the role and it's been an amazing journey. It's allowed me to serve others and discover my true purpose in this life.

I think the fact that I've had to overcome a lot of big challenges in my life has made me exceptionally strong and resilient. I see other people who, even at the first sign of adversity, get thrown off their rockers. But when I experience adversity, I just get up, dust myself off and keep moving forward.

When it comes to dealing with your past, you have two choices. Either you can allow your past to make you or you can allow your past to break you. I was determined to not be broken. I learned as a young child that my future and my happiness was up to me. That's why I worked hard in school and made good grades. I participated in every sport and every organization that I could possibly participate in, in order to get as many scholarships as possible, so that I could leave the state of Mississippi and begin a new life somewhere else.

And so, I learned at a young age that it's all in your mindset. If you believe that you can do something, you can, even when you're facing a traumatic situation. You can resolve any problem if you make up your mind to do it. When you get tired of being sick and tired, you'll make the necessary changes. I learned as a child that I was in control of my own happiness. No one else. You've got to go out there and create your own happiness, and then share it with others. If you depend on others to bring you that happiness, it will only result in pain and disappointment.

I want to be able to look in the mirror and say to myself that I am somebody, and that I deserve the best that life has to offer. And I want to know that when I look in that mirror, I won't feel like crying because I don't like who I see. I want to be happy with the image that's looking back at me. That's important to me. So, the first step is to change the mindset, so that the person who I see in the mirror makes me happy because I'm looking at the person that God wants me to be.

The biggest lesson I've learned in my life is the value and power of forgiveness, and the impact it has had on me and others in my life. Thank you, Lord, for giving me the strength to forgive.

About
MARK HOLLAND

In 2020, after 27 years of service, Mark retired from Pastoring Kingdom First Ministries, a Non-Denominational Church which he founded with his wife, Dr. Michelle Holland. They have two beautiful daughters, Amanda Christine Holland - 22, and Kimberly Faith Holland - 20.

His undergraduate studies were completed in 1989 with a Bachelor of Science in Building Construction Technology from Hampton University in Hampton, VA. He subsequently went on to complete his Masters and Doctoral Degrees in Ministry in 1995 from Family Bible Institute, College and Seminary in Baltimore, MD.

In 1889 he also earned his Commission as a Second Lieutenant in the US Army, where he served in the US Army National Guard until exiting with an honorable discharge on January 1, 2003 to survivors.

Chapter 2
"Shaped by love and loss: Persist Until Success Happens [PUSH]"

www.drmarkholland.com

SHAPED BY LOVE AND LOSS:
PERSIST UNTIL SUCCESS HAPPENS (PUSH)

MARK HOLLAND

Has life ever thrown you a curveball, and you weren't sure how to move forward? A curveball is one of the hardest pitches to hit in baseball and when life throws one, it can be one of the biggest obstacles to overcome. For me, those moments came early and often, but they were instrumental in helping me turn my life around and point me toward my right path.

I grew up in Baltimore, Maryland, the youngest of five children. Our family had its share of struggles, but luckily for me, we also had an abundance of love. My mother was my first hero. I've never met anyone with more strength or resilience. She was the rock that held us all together, working tirelessly to provide for us after my father left.

But even with her unwavering support, life had a way of knocking us down. When I was just a child, my brother Walt died in a car accident. He was a towering figure in my life, a seven-foot-tall gentle giant with dreams of playing in the NBA. His loss was devastating to all of us and he left a void that could never be filled.

Tragedy struck my family again when my sister Kim, the most loving person I've ever known, took her own life. She had struggled with a chemical imbalance her entire life, and in a moment of darkness, she made a decision that changed the shape of our family forever. The hole left in our family after losing her was almost unbearable. It is a wound that never fully heals.

Finding Solace in the Unexpected

While I mourned the loss of my siblings, I also found myself at a crossroads. I was attending Coppin State University, just a mile from my old high school stomping grounds, on an ROTC and track scholarship. But I was struggling. I was unable to focus on my studies because it felt as though the weight of my losses were pulling me under in a riptide of despair. I needed a lifeline. Someone to help me find my way out of the darkness because I couldn't see a path out myself.

That lifeline came in the form of an unexpected phone call with my father. When he left us, our relationship became almost non-existent. But, at that moment, it was as though he knew I needed someone to listen, to understand the pain I was going through. And to my surprise, he did more than just listen. I shared with him that I was thinking of changing schools because I needed to start over but I was hesitating. Even though I was in pain in my current situation, I was scared to make a change.

My father listened to me talk about the problems I was facing at school and asked, "Well, what do you want to do about it?" When I told him I was thinking of transferring, he immediately offered to take me the next day to check out the new college I was considering. He gave me the push I needed to do something about my situation and make the change I knew was best for me. That phone call helped me correct the course of my life. It also showed me that we are not taking leaps in the dark. Faith protects us all, especially when we're afraid.

Together, my dad and I drove down to Hampton University, an historically Black college in Virginia. As soon as I set foot on campus, I knew I had found my new home. It seemed like a place of possibility, a chance to start over and build a future that wasn't defined by my past.

But making change is never easy, is it? I had already started classes at Coppin, and the thought of leaving behind everything I knew was terrifying. Although I may not have been happy, I was at least in a place of comfort. I knew what to expect. But deep down I understood that if I kept doing the same things, I would always get the same result. I needed to make a change. So with my father's encouragement, I found the courage to take a chance.

Stepping Out of My Comfort Zone

Think about the last time you had to make a difficult decision. Remember that nauseous feeling in the pit of your stomach as you stepped out of your comfort zone and into the unknown? That's exactly how I felt when I transferred to Hampton. This wasn't just about changing schools; this was about changing the trajectory of my life.

Because I knew that if I stayed at Coppin, I would be stuck in the same cycle of pain and loss that had defined my childhood. I needed a fresh start, a chance to break free from the ghosts of my past and build a future that was entirely my own.

So, even though I knew it was the right choice, there was a lot of fear mixed in with excitement when I withdrew from Coppin and prepared to start again at Hampton. But I believed in my heart that this decision would set me on a better path toward purpose, passion, and fulfillment.

Looking back, I realize that phone call with my father was a turning point, a moment when someone saw my potential and refused to let me settle for less. It introduced me to the power of mentorship, of having someone in your corner who believes in you even when you don't believe in yourself.

When the Party Ends: A Wake-Up Call

As I settled into life at Hampton, I found myself caught up in the excitement of my new surroundings. For the first time, I was truly on my own, free to make my own choices and chart my own course. And, just like many young folk who finally have a taste of freedom, I started to make mistakes. Little did I know that all the freedom I was enjoying was about to test my resolve and force me to confront the consequences of my actions.

Like many, I found myself more focused on the social scene than on my studies during my freshman year. I was pledging a fraternity, attending parties, and living life to the fullest. But as the semester wore on, I realized that I was also neglecting the very reason I had come to Hampton in the first place: to get an education.

And that neglect took a toll. Instead of a 4.0, I had a measly 1.9. When I received my grades at the end of the semester, it hit me like a ton of bricks. I was devastated, knowing that I had let myself down and jeopardized the new chance that had been given to me.

A Moment of Truth

Fortunately for me, my poor academic performance didn't go unnoticed. I say fortunately because when Colonel Foy, the head of the ROTC department at Hampton, called me into his office, he gave me a wake-up call I sorely needed.

As I sat across from him, my heart racing, he asked me a simple question: "Do you like it here, son?" I nodded, unable to find the words to express how much Hampton meant to me. What he said next would stay with me forever.

"Let me make a promise to you," he said, his voice

stern but not unkind. "If you come in my office under these circumstances again, you won't be here."

At that moment, I realized the gravity of my situation. I had been given an incredible opportunity, one that many people would have given anything for. But I was on the verge of throwing it all away.

The Road to Redemption: AKA Putting in the Work

The road to redemption starts with a first step. As Les says, "It's not over until you decide it is! No matter what the obstacle and challenge, you can overcome it." I knew if I wanted to be successful at Hampton, I would need to let go of old habits and embrace a new way of being.

My meeting with Colonel Foy put into sharp focus just how out of hand I had let things get. But it also gave me the kick in the butt I needed to get my act together. If I wanted to stay at Hampton, I had to get serious about my studies. I had to put in the work, day in and day out, no matter how difficult it seemed. So that's exactly what I did.

I cut back on socializing, focusing instead on my classes and my future. I studied harder than I ever had before, determined to prove to myself and everyone else that I belonged at Hampton.

Slowly but surely, my grades began to improve. I went from barely passing to making the Dean's List. To see my hard work and dedication pay off was one of my proudest moments. But more than that, it reminded me of the importance of staying true to oneself and one's dreams, of not getting lost in the distractions of the moment.

Breaking the Cycle

We often don't realize the impact our own success can have on those around us. But as I began to thrive at Hampton, I realized that my journey was about more than just myself. It was about paving the way for others. The ability to overcome my past and thrive could show others that no matter where they came from, they too could achieve their dreams.

As a young African American male from Baltimore, I knew all too well the challenges that many of my peers faced. I had lost too many friends and family members to the streets. I have had my heart broken as promising lives were cut short by violence and despair.

But I refused to let that be my story. I was determined to break the cycle, to show that there was another way. And as I walked across the stage at my graduation, my degree in hand, I knew that I had done just that.

Building a Life of Purpose

Have you ever felt a calling, a deep sense of purpose that seems to guide you every step of your journey? For me, that calling came in the form of ministry. I am driven by a deep desire to share the love and grace that has transformed my own life.

It started after graduating from Hampton when I found myself drawn to the church. During those services, the seed of an idea to help others navigate the challenges and triumphs of life was planted. And once the desire to help others took root, I found myself called to make another huge step forward in my life: I entered the world of pastoral ministry.

But my journey was not meant to be a solitary one. During my time at Hampton, I met the love of my life, Michelle. She was a beacon of light that instantly drew me to her. What I didn't know then is that Michelle would be a source of strength and encouragement that would sustain me through the ups and downs of the life we would build together.

And what a life it is. Together, we have created a life of purpose. We founded Kingdom First Ministries and have poured our hearts into the community we served for 27 years. It has been our privilege to walk alongside our congregation, sharing in their joys and sorrows, their victories and defeats.

Overcoming Challenges Together

Think about the relationships that have changed your life. Are there people who have stood by your side through thick and thin? For Michelle and me, our marriage was not just a personal connection; it was a partnership in purpose, a shared commitment to making a difference in the world.

But that doesn't mean it was always easy. Like any couple, we faced our share of challenges. We have had moments when it seemed like we were speaking different languages. And the first year of our marriage felt like everything was falling apart.

We argued constantly. We weren't just on different pages. We were in different books, both of us convinced that we were right and the other was wrong. It was a trying time that tested the very foundation of our relationship. Looking back, it was our faith, our shared belief in God, that not only brought us together but kept us together.

And slowly but surely, we began to find our way. We learned how to communicate. We figured out how to listen to each other's perspectives and find common ground. We discovered that the key to a strong marriage was not perfection, but partnership. And Michelle and I are committed to working together even when things get tough.

The Powerful Foundation of Love

As our marriage grew stronger, so too did our family. Michelle and I were blessed with two incredible daughters, Amanda and Kimberly. They are the light of our lives and not to get too soppy here (they would hate that), they are truly the embodiment of all our hopes and dreams.

Don't get me wrong, raising our kids was not without its challenges. We struggled to balance the demands of ministry with the needs of our family. It was quite a learning curve to figure out how to have time for both our calling and our kids. I felt like I was constantly juggling. And there were times where I felt like I was failing both the church and my family.

But throughout it all, we prioritized our children. Michelle and I worked to create a home that was filled with love, laughter, and learning. We wanted to give them the tools we never had growing up. Our goal was that when they were ready to chase their dreams, they would be set up for success.

And as I have watched them grow into the tremendous human beings they are, I realize that part of the greatest legacy we will leave is love. My daughters know that they are valued and that their lives have meaning and purpose. The man I am today was built on the foundation of love for my family.

Transition and Transformation

Luckily, my time at Hampton taught me to embrace change because I recently found myself once again at a crossroads. After 27 years in pastoral ministry, I have a new stirring in my heart. It is the feeling that God is calling me to something new.

But thinking about leaving my role in the community I helped build seemed like an impossible decision. Not only that, but I would once again need to step out of my comfort zone and into the unknown. But now that I'm older, I know I can't ignore the prompting of my heart.

See, I once had a cross-country coach who taught me that when you're in an event, always run 10 yards through the finish line. Meaning, don't relax before or even at the finish line. To successfully finish the race (and win), you need to see something all the way through. I have always had a calling to help others and I often use the story of my life to do that.

And so to run through the finish line of my ministry, I now need to share my story even further, and reach even more people. To do this, I have retired from my role as pastor and have embarked on a new journey as an author and speaker. And just as before, this was a transition that would test my faith and my resilience but would allow me to achieve my life's purpose.

Embracing a New Calling

I had always been a storyteller, using my sermons to paint pictures of hope and resilience. But now, I wanted to share those stories with a wider audience. And while it was exciting to think about reaching a larger community, it was also daunting. It felt vulnerable to put to page the tragedies and triumphs of my past. It felt scary to speak out loud to a room full of strangers about the strength I found to turn my life around. But I knew that I could not let fear control me. Just as I had when I changed schools and then again when I built my church, I would need to take a leap of faith and trust in the path that God had laid out for me.

And so, I began to write. I poured my heart onto the page, sharing the struggles and triumphs that had shaped my life. I spoke about the power of perseverance, the importance of family, and the transformative nature of faith.

Empowering Others to Overcome

As I wrote, I began to realize the true power of sharing our stories. Since becoming an author, I have received messages from readers all over the world, people who had been touched by my story and inspired to make changes in their own lives.

Some had faced similar challenges, battling addiction or struggling to find their place in the world. Others were simply looking for a message of hope, a reminder that they too could overcome the obstacles in their path and start anew.

And with each message, each story of transformation, I feel a renewed sense of purpose. I understand that my story is not just about me, but about the countless lives that can be changed through the power of sharing our experiences.

Looking back to my own childhood, from my mother and her strength in raising a family on her own to Colonel Foy who wouldn't let a young man throw away his future, I feel fortunate to have the mentors and role models I've had who helped me find my path.

I remember the impact my father had when I lacked the courage to chase my dreams. I want to be that same kind of influence. I want to use my story to empower others to break free from the cycles of pain and limitation that often hold them back.

Leaving a Legacy

I am at a place in my life where I am contemplating my legacy. And as I reflect on my journey, I realize the pain I have experienced offers some of the greatest gifts. The fire of loss forged me into the person I was meant to become.

But, it has also given me a unique perspective. One that has given me a way of connecting with others who have faced similar struggles. I am able to see the potential in people, even when they can't see it in themselves.

Some of the young people I have mentored over the years have come from broken homes and tough neighborhoods like myself. But I now have the ability to see past their circumstances to their possibility. It's as though my superpower is the ability to find the light in their eyes and zero in on their hunger for something more.

My purpose in life is to help them find their way, to show them that their past does not have to dictate their future. I want to be a reminder to others like me that, no matter where they came from, they have the power to create a life of meaning and purpose.

Living Life On Purpose

As I look back on my life, I am filled with a sense of gratitude and awe. I have been blessed beyond measure, given opportunities that I never could have imagined as a child growing up in Baltimore. I have been given a chance to make a difference, using my own story to inspire and empower others.

I don't know what the future holds, what challenges and triumphs lie ahead. But I do know that I will face them with the same faith and resilience that have carried me this far.

And I hope my story serves as inspiration to the kids out there who may be hurting or doubting their own potential. No matter where we come from, we all have the power to make a new choice and take a new path toward our true purpose. Because in the end, that's what it's all about. LIfe is not about the accolades or the achievements, but about the lives we touch along the way. It's about leaving this world a little better than we found it, one story at a time.

ABOUT

Dr. Eliyahu Shmuel Ben Yah

Dr. Eliyahu Shmuel Ben Yah is an accomplished author, highly spirited, anointed, passionate, dynamic speaker. He has traveled both nationally within the US and to several countries, and has written 17 books all dealing with spiritual matters. Dr. Eliyahu is a former correctional officer working in law enforcement in Texas and is currently a HPD (Houston, TX) & Fort Bend Sheriff Department Chaplain, holding religious services at TDCJ once a week. In his role as Rabbi he has dealt with people from all walks of life, which led him to further his studies, concentrating in the area of health. During his journey to study psychology, and to obtain his associates degree, he chose an elective in hypnotherapy and holistic practices, subsequently becoming an herbalist. He followed this by studying for his PhD in the same field.He is a singer, community activist, life, mental and spiritual coach, holistic practitioner.

Chapter 3
"From desperation to
dedication: a leap of faith"

https://esbyah.blogspot.com
and www.amazon.com/author/
eliyahushmuel

 Eliyahu Shmuel Ben Yah

 navi_of_yahweh

 www.esbyah.blogspot.com

FROM DESPERATION TO DEDICATION: A LEAP OF FAITH

DR. ELIYAHU SHMUEL BEN YAH

In my life, my hero was my father, a man whose devotion to his family and work ethic was nothing short of extraordinary. Imagine a man juggling three jobs, yet never missing a beat when it came to spending quality time with his loved ones. That was my father. He was the very picture of responsibility and restraint—I can't recall a single instance of him smoking, drinking, or speaking ill of anyone. He was more than just a provider; he was the moral compass of our home.

My father wore many hats: he was a superintendent, a painter, and a plumber, and he held a full-time job at the port in the bustling heart of New York City. Yet, he always found the energy for us, often fuelling himself with a careful blend of vitamins and minerals to keep up with the demands of his life. His downtime was sacred, but even then, he'd invite me along for a motorcycle ride, teaching me lessons about life in the process. "Hold on tight, and don't resist the turns," he'd say, a metaphor that later I would come to appreciate in more ways than one.

He saw potential in me, urging me to read, to learn, to be more. He believed I was destined for something unique, and though he wasn't the most openly affectionate man, his old-school ways of showing love were through acts of service and quiet affirmations.

As a child, my ambitions oscillated between becoming a teacher and serving as a police officer. I was hungry for knowledge, hated ignorance, and had a relentless curiosity that I now recognize as a gift. A teacher once told me, "The only dumb question is the one you don't ask," and that advice has been etched into my soul ever since.

Today, I may not stand in a secular classroom or walk a beat as an officer, but I have found my calling as a teacher of sorts. I share wisdom through the teachings of the Bible, and my experiences as a former correctional officer and chaplain have given me a unique platform to educate and inspire.

Seeking Refuge: By Exile and Return

But my tale is not without its shadows. My father, a man, who was in his third marriage brought me into a new family dynamic where I often felt like the odd one out—a "sacrificial lamb," if you will. For years, I grappled with the confusing messages and actions of my father, a man whose words were scarce yet weighted with significance. The rarity of times he said "*I love you*" made them precious, sustaining me through the toughest periods, despite the turmoil churning within me.

The truth about my parentage remained a secret until I turned 14; the woman I believed to be my mother was in fact my step- mother. This discovery sent me spiraling into a pit of despair so deep that I considered ending my life. But it was the belief in my father's love that kept me tethered to hope.

My stepmother's treatment of me was nothing short of abuse. She could be at times abusive—physically, emotionally, mentally—and in a bid for peace, I was sent away to Chicago between the ages of five to ten. There, I faced unspeakable harm at the hands of my cousin, who molested me, and when I reached out for help, I was dismissed by my father, who couldn't deal with my return.

The years were marred by a barrage of insults and physical pain that left deep scars, not only on my skin but on my soul. "You're stupid, you're ugly, look at your ears they're so big, you'll never amount to anything," the words echoed, while the beatings from electric cables served as a brutal punctuation to each cruel sentence. My father, though not the hand behind the punishment, was the silent spectator to my suffering.

At 10 years old I returned home, but that didn't last very long. I was sent to live with my grandmother in Puerto Rico. It was this phenomenal woman who saved me from committing suicide. My grandmother recognized the desperation in my eyes and intervened just as I stood on the precipice of ending it all. She became my savior, my guardian angel who pulled me back from the edge with her unwavering prayers.

My life was deeply rooted in the church. It was in this environment that I learned a powerful lesson: family is the cornerstone of life, and no matter how you're treated, the key to triumph is to counter evil with goodness, to disarm hostility with kindness. But one must be shrewd—for kindness without wisdom can lead to being taken advantage of. It's about finding balance, about enduring the storm to see what truly holds value.

Through the passage of time and the pursuit of knowledge, I've come to understand and forgive both my father and stepmother for their actions. Our relationship, healed and whole, became a source of strength until my father's last breath. When he passed away, I was free from guilt, for I respected the man he was—the fighter, the survivor.

A Mask of Sobriety: The Facade

There was a time when the church offered little in the way of guidance beyond spiritual advice. As a young soul in search of direction, I yearned for more than what they provided. It's like the wisdom found in Deuteronomy 22, which teaches us not to mix seeds and expect them to flourish together. The church sowed seeds of prayer, respect, and honor within us, but they didn't equip us with the tools to make wise decisions in life. This was the way back then; now, thankfully, churches have evolved to offer more comprehensive support.

My journey led me away from Puerto Rico. The year was a blur between 1987 and 1989, and I found myself yearning for more than what my homeland could offer. I was seeking a fresh start because life seemed stagnant.

My emotional foundation was shaky, and after moving back from Puerto Rico to Brooklyn following Hurricane Hugo, I sought solace with my father. I attempted to open up to the pastor about my struggles, hoping for understanding and support. However, one day, I overheard a conversation that shattered my trust. The pastor mentioned my father's generous donations to the church, implying that my well-being was only important because of the financial benefits they received.

That moment was a turning point for me. I had always carried my faith proudly, known in my neighborhood as a devout Christian. But hearing those words from the pastor made me question the authenticity of their concern for me. It felt as though my value to the church was measured in monetary terms, not by my faith or my character.

Suddenly, I found myself questioning everything I had once stood for, everything I had preached. It was a downward spiral that seemed to pull me deeper with each passing day. I put away my Bible and for the next two and a half years, I turned away from my calling and fell into the darkness of addiction. I wandered off the path, lost in a haze of drugs and alcohol, trapped in the embrace of addiction from the tender age of 17 until the cusp of 21. I knew I was lucky to celebrate every passing birthday and Christmas, not knowing if I'd be alive for the next one. I sought to silence the divine whispers and my conscience with drugs and alcohol. Despite growing up in the church, I did a complete 180, transforming from a devoted believer to someone unrecognizable.

Even as I held down a job at Memorial Sloan Kettering Cancer Center, my life was in shambles. I was a high-functioning alcoholic—always cheerful and efficient at work, but it was all an act fueled by my addiction. One day, my supervisor noticed my struggle. In a discreet act of kindness, he handed me $20 and told me to "get a fix" so I could keep functioning. That's how low I had sunk, relying on malt liquor and eventually cocaine just to get through each day.

My addiction escalated from malt liquor to hard liquor, to the point where I was consuming four bottles a day. I even turned to cocaine, from my cousin who was a corrupt police officer. We partied hard, and the substance became another escape from reality. The spiral continued until I decided to leave home. I was living wherever the night took me, often passing out from drinking too much.

Awakening of Intuition: Discovering a Prophetic Gift

I have always possessed a heightened sense of perception – a prophetic intuition if you will. The gifts we are bestowed with come without a requirement for restitution; they are ours to steward and eventually, we must answer for how we've managed them. Yet, there was a time when I didn't recognize the extent of my gifts, my shattered confidence made me doubt my abilities. I was taught to pray about my problems, with little emphasis on counseling or mentorship. It was an oversight that would later come into play in the most unexpected of ways.

Remarkably, it was during a period of indulgence in alcohol that my dormant gift seemed to stir. I recall one incident vividly: I was at a bar when a woman, Denzing Abenham, struck up a conversation with me. Half Puerto Rican, half Jewish, she had a sharp wit about her.

"You're the religious type, huh?" she prodded, a hint of curiosity in her voice.

Caught off guard, I blurted out, "Oh, snap!" My mind raced – here I was, a preacher, sipping wine in a bar. "Who here knows me?" I wondered aloud.

"Don't worry," Denzing reassured me with a dismissive wave. "I have no idea who you are."

We exchanged a few more words, and it was clear she found it unusual for someone like me to be in a bar. But as we talked, something within me ignited—a prophetic insight. I turned to her and said, "My dear, you're facing a legal problem." The words flowed from me, unbidden. "In fact, when you were just 14, a family member sexually abused and raped you, leaving scars too deep for children of your own."

Her eyes widened in shock, but before she could respond, a young man nearby piped up, eager for a taste of this truth-telling. I tried to explain that it didn't work on command—it was more of an inspired moment. Yet, he insisted.

"All I need is another glass of that red wine," I joked, trying to lighten the mood. But as I peered into his future, the humor faded. "My friend, what I see isn't pleasant. If you don't turn your heart towards God within the next 30 days, you will die."

His casual demeanor dropped, replaced by a sad realization. "That's not good news," he acknowledged.

I could only nod, feeling the weight of my words. "It's what I've been given to share. No more, no less."

A month later, I returned to that very bar, only to find the patrons awaiting my arrival. The bartender refused my money, his face solemn. "The crowd's here for you," he explained. "Your predictions... they've come true."

The young man I had spoken to had not lived to see the 30 days. A tragic accident had claimed his life on the fourth day. This revelation brought me to tears, and a fear of the gift I possessed settled over me. That day, I left the bar with a heavy heart, vowing to approach my gift with the reverence and caution it deserved.

Another time, at a gathering a while back, my cousin, a police officer, had an extravagant display on his table: a mountain of cocaine and an array of bottles. The atmosphere was charged, and in that haze, I found myself with a heightened sense of clarity. Turning to a young Italian girl named Tony Anne at the party, I spoke with a conviction that surprised even me.

"Tony Anne," I said, looking into her eyes, "you've got 20 pills in your bag. You're planning to end your life after tonight. You know this path doesn't lead to heaven, and I can see evil spirits mocking you." Tears welled up in her eyes as the truth of my words hit home.

Then there was Robin, a Jewish girl at the party. "Robin," I questioned, "why do I envision you lying on a couch, tears streaming down your face?" I described a man to her, and she gasped, "Oh my God, that's my father!" The story unfolded of how he had molested her, leading to her parents' divorce, and the guilt she harbored. "God has forgiven you," I assured her, "and He will restore what's been broken."

Despite my intoxication, these revelations flowed through me. The girls at the party were moved, shedding tears as I spoke truths into their lives. But not everyone was pleased. My cousin and brother grew angry, their irritation clear. "Every time you drink, you start preaching about God," they complained. "Just go back to church. You don't belong here."

These outbursts didn't deter me. Even with the chaos around me, I was acutely aware of my protection. I had faced guns and danger, yet a voice within always guided me to safety. "Don't go there, turn here," it would say, and I would listen, narrowly avoiding trouble.

As was my habit, I drank to the point of blacking out. I would always carry a backpack with a change of clothes and toothpaste, prepared for wherever the night might leave me. The next morning, no matter where I awoke, I would get up, shower, and head to work as if nothing had happened.

The Call to Preaching

It was a night like any other when I returned home, weary and confused. My father, witnessing my disheveled state, was full of concern. "What happened?" he asked. I brushed off his inquiries, my mind clouded with exhaustion. "I don't want to talk about it," I replied. "I just need to sleep."

A vivid dream unfolded before me. I was standing in a field, drawn towards an enormous barn that seemed to stretch endlessly like a cathedral of the plains. A familiar hymn, "How Great Thou Art," filled the air, sung in English with such passion that it stirred my very soul. Curiosity piqued, I moved closer, discovering that the barn was a colossal stadium filled with preachers I recognized from days gone by. Icons like Oral Roberts, T.L. Osborn, A.A. Allen, and Kathryn Kuhlman were present, with R.W. Schambach serving as the master of ceremonies.

I listened as Schambach's voice boomed through the stadium, "Ladies and gentlemen, we have a man of God here ready to preach the gospel. Let's welcome him with a round of applause!" The spotlight turned to me, and panic set in. Clad only in a T-shirt and jeans, I felt unworthy, a backslider who had no right to stand before these giants of faith. Then, to my astonishment, the very pastor who had ridiculed me years before approached me. With a gesture of forgiveness and unity, he draped his jacket over my shoulders and handed me his Bible. "You don't realize the honor you've been given to preach the gospel," he said. Tears streamed down my face as I backed away, overwhelmed by a sense of inadequacy. "No, I can't," I protested, until the dream shattered, and I awoke on Sunday morning, my cheeks still wet with tears.

Confused by the days, I asked my father when the next church service was. He suggested I visit my uncle's church, where a revival was underway with a guest preacher named Val Melendez. "They're preaching under the title, 'God is looking for a few good men,'" my father said. I arrived with a heart open to God's message, remembering the title more than the sermon itself. "God, talk to me," I prayed, hoping for clarity. As the preacher finished, I felt an urge I couldn't resist—I ran forward, amidst the crying congregation, seeking to rededicate my heart to God. Doubts crept in, whispered by the devil's voice, suggesting my actions were mere religious emotion, a reaction to the dream. But as hands were laid upon me, a voice of welcome cut through, "Welcome back, son. Heaven has been waiting for you; you're one of the few good men." And with that, the preacher stepped back, disappearing through a door, leaving me with a renewed sense of purpose and a place among those called to serve.

During that year I crossed paths with Steven Galloza, a young man who would later become a psychologist with his practice in Florida. Steven was like an angel in my life, assisting me through the maze of my emotions, the bitterness, and the resentment that I harbored. Our friendship blossomed, and we became not just roommates but brothers in spirit. Eventually, I had the honor of being his best man.

Together, we embarked on a daring mission trip to Cuba in 1994. While in Cuba for 41 days, I served as interpreter for Rev. Shaeffer, a former Rabbi and whose background was fascinating; they owned the Schaefer Beer Company. He was raised as a rabbi but had converted to Christianity. During our mission, I served as his Spanish interpreter, which marked the beginning of my journey in ministry. After 41 days in Cuba, my life took another unexpected turn. I left my job at Memorial and took a position that juggled the roles of a paralegal, process server, and mail clerk for the law firm Watson Farley and Williams, which specialized in international taxation and import-export law, located in downtown Manhattan.

It was here that I met Eugene Jimenez, whose brother, RaymondoJimenez, was a pioneer in radio broadcasting in California and one of the first Puerto Rican evangelists from the Assemblies of God. They were trailblazers, even entering Russia to preach the gospel before it was open to evangelists like Billy Graham. Eugene had a global reach, and whenever he visited Puerto Rico, he'd summon me. I'd assist him, ironing his clothes, praying for him, and helping sell his books and other materials at events. His influence was immense, and when I encountered him unexpectedly, the youth pastor at my church recognized him as a renowned international evangelist.

The senior pastor, Luciano Padilla, inquired about me, and Eugene introduced me enthusiastically, recounting tales of my fiery preaching in Puerto Rico. I felt a flush of embarrassment, remembering my period of backsliding, but I was humbled by the warm welcome.

Surprisingly, Pastor Padilla revealed that during his early morning prayers, God had instructed him to find a young man to serve as an interpreter for the visiting former rabbi. I was chosen for this role, much to the delight of my friend Stephen, who saw it as a sign of God's continuing purpose for my life. Though I tried to downplay the significance, insisting I was merely an interpreter, not a preacher, I accepted the call.

The hardest part was approaching my employer, as I had just returned from vacation and exhausted all my sick days. Would they understand the urgency of this divine appointment?

As I sat in my office, the quiet was pierced by a voice that seemed to come from nowhere. It was so clear, so direct, that I couldn't ignore it. The voice led me to Karen Miller, our office administrator—a woman of Irish and Italian descent, a Catholic with a kind heart.

"Karen," I started, unsure how to explain what I was about to say. "I believe I've just heard something from God. You and your husband have been trying for a baby for 10 years, with no success. You've faced the heartache of miscarriages, and doctors have urged you to give up hope of having your own child. But, Karen, I feel compelled to tell you that God has a different plan. Tear up those adoption papers. By this time next year, you will be blessed with a son."

Tears filled her eyes, and soon we were both crying—overwhelmed by the promise of a miracle. As I turned to leave, she stopped me, reminding me that I hadn't yet asked for the favor I came for.

"Karen, I need to take a leave of absence," I confessed. "God has called me to go to Cuba to preach and to serve as an interpreter. I'll be bringing books and clothing to those in need."

When I returned from Cuba 41 days later, Karen greeted me with incredible news—she was pregnant. But four months in, she faced another trial. She called me into her office, her voice trembling with fear.

"I'm bleeding," she said. "The doctors are advising me to consider an abortion. They don't believe the baby will make it."

"Karen, listen to me," I said. "Place your hand on your belly and simply say 'Thank you, Jesus.' No need for elaborate prayers or pleas to the saints. Just 'Thank you, God.' That's all."

Months later, Karen proudly introduced her baby boy, Christian Matthew Miller. Her husband, filled with gratitude, pulled me aside and offered a gesture of his thanks, willing to write me a check for any amount up to $10,000.

I was moved to tears but refused, "I can't accept your money. Instead, I ask one thing of you—take Christian to a church filled with the Holy Spirit, one that preaches the true Gospel."

Reflecting on that moment, I realized the power of faith and the importance of purifying and dedicating one's gifts to God. I had offered my gift back to Him, asking for nothing in return but His sanctification.

The Divine Directive: A New Chapter

I moved from Brooklyn to the Bronx, wrestling with questions about my purpose. Should I continue serving God or pursue a different path? During this time, I was still working at the law firm, searching for direction. Then, clear as day, God's message came to me. He wanted me to commit to full-time ministry.

I followed that call, pastoring in Holyoke, Massachusetts, for two years, and then in Naples, Florida, for a year and a half. I left behind a pastor in Naples who expanded our efforts to the Netherlands, creating a legacy of 13 churches.

During this mission, God promised to show me the woman who would become my wife. Unlike my past relationships, where I hadn't sought God's guidance, this time I earnestly prayed for His choice. My parents were no longer part of my life, leaving me to navigate these choices without their input.

Then, at a church where I was preaching—a church my future wife wasn't even a member of—our paths crossed. Led by a feeling in her spirit, she accompanied her mother to that very service. The church was filled with single women, and one even boldly invited me to dinner, claiming God had told her we were meant for each other.

However, it was Stephen Galloza who through writing via text pointed out the right woman. He said to me, "That woman there, she's the one from the Lord. She will bring healing and redemption to your life, refine you, and you'll do the same for her. You're going to have a wonderful life together."

My first marriage blessed me with two older children, and now I share my two younger children with my wife. This journey has been nothing short of amazing. My feet have touched the soils of Cuba, the Philippines—not once, but thrice—Vietnam, London, France, and the vibrant cultures of South and Central America. I've even ventured to the Dominican Republic, Cuba again, and Canada.

But life isn't just about the places you visit; it's about the trials you overcome. When I met my wife, my finances took an unexpected dive. You see, I embraced the Hebrew roots of my faith, and suddenly, I was labeled. People thought I was turning to Judaism, and just like that, doors slammed shut. I was a busy speaker, always on the go, but the invitations dried up. They called me a false prophet, a heretic. And the result? Homelessness.

Imagine, in the cold underbelly of Lorain, Ohio, my pregnant wife and I huddled in a basement, a place barely fit to be called a home. I reached out to friends, shared photos, videos—anything to show the harshness of our reality. I sought work relentlessly. And through those tough months, a few kind souls sent us offerings, for which we were grateful. Prayer became our refuge; tears, our language. A verse clung to my heart: "I was young and now I am old, yet I have never seen the righteous forsaken."

In my darkest hour, I cried out, "God, why? I've been

honorable, I've stayed true. What's the reason for my suffering?" And that's when it came to me, a question from the heavens: "What can you do better than most?" The answer? Teach. So, I started a foundation in 2014, a place for thought and prophets to flourish.

I've always had a passion for writing, and with the birth of social media, I found an outlet for my voice. With my wife's support - I wasn't just computer savvy - I became an author. In just one year, I penned 10 books. It was through these works that I clawed my way out of poverty. We secured an apartment and a car—finally, we had what we needed to live.

Slowly but surely, trust was rebuilt. I leveraged social platforms, but again, suspicion arose. Pastors were wary, thinking I had become a Hebrew Israelite. I had to clarify: "No, absolutely not. I'm rooted in Hebrew tradition, not Judaism."

I've been blessed with unwavering support from my Messianic Rabbi, and a circle of friends who often seek my counsel, especially on matters of marriage. They value my understanding of Hebrew and Greek, frequently asking for insights or references when they're grappling with life's challenges. This has led me to nurture a virtual congregation, which I'm excited to say will soon transition into a physical one this February.

My wife has become a cornerstone of our community as well—a public notary and a tax preparer. Together, we serve as chaplains, offering guidance and support to those in need.

In the realm of writing, I've recently collaborated on a book, sharing the authorship spotlight. And, driven by a deep love for reading, I penned a book celebrating my little daughter's artistic talents. She's a budding artist, and I'm always engaged in something, whether it's writing or reading. My wife and I challenge ourselves to read about three books each month, exchanging ideas and insights. We sit down and discuss our thoughts, and I meticulously jot down the key points in a notebook. If one of us is intrigued by the other's book, we'll swap and read it.

My days are filled with counseling and coaching, as I am a life coach, mental health coach, and holistic practitioner. This has allowed me to cultivate an audience that seeks my guidance, even here in Houston where I plan to establish a ministry—a teaching ministry focused on nurturing successors and evangelists. I believe that the role of the evangelist has been undervalued and wish to restore its significance. In my eyes, true spiritual leadership is about winning souls, empowering people, and sharing enlightenment. Without these, one risks creating a cult, not a community.

I embarked on my formal studies later in life, earning two doctorates in divinity and undergoing extensive chaplaincy training. I'm currently working towards a degree in philosophy and psychology from Queen's College and will complete my Ph.D. next year. At 51, I stand as a testament that it's never too late to pursue knowledge and make a difference.

I want to leave you with this, embrace your relentless ambitions. Passionately promote who you are and what you stand for, without a hint of half-heartedness. Cherish those who celebrate your path, and surround yourself with people who honor your destiny and your mission. Distance yourself from negativity: Seek the company of those who uplift rather than bring you down and avoid those who harbor ill will. Jealousy and envy are forms of animosity that can distort relationships. It's crucial to recognize and steer clear of such destructive emotions - the power of life is in the spoken word, so choose your words wisely and fill your circle with those who will challenge and inspire you.

Remember, the roadblocks you encounter are not setbacks but affirmations that you're on the right path. The struggles you face will only deepen your appreciation and understanding of your achievements. Value every step, for it is in the journey that we find our true strength. Let us move forward with love, both for ourselves and for those around us, and may our words always be a source of positive change.

ABOUT

ABOUT
KELLY FAULKENBERY

Kelly is married to Corbett, the love of her life. They have been blessed with 4 children and a granddaughter, Maxine. She rejoices in her love of Jesus and her heart is happiest cheering on others to encounter their true identity in Jesus and equipping others to live out all they were created to be. When not working at their family business, she loves grabbing every opportunity - be it in her hometown of Waco, Tx, or throughout the United States or abroad - to go and be His hands and feet.

Along with their tribe, they have been blessed to serve in Peru, Costa Rica, Colombia, Africa, Canada and Haiti. They have witnessed miracle after miracle healings, deliverance, and people encountering the Presence of God, falling in love with Jesus. Whether sharing stories from behind the podium or in the dirt, her heart song is that every woman of the world embrace their true identity and encounter the all-encompassing love of Jesus.

Chapter 4
"Life and death stakes"

 Kelly Faulkenbery

 kellyfaulkenbery

 www.kellyfaulkenbery.com

LIFE AND DEATH STAKES

KELLY FAULKENBERY

**Founder of He Sees You Ministries and Author of
Hey Girl, He Sees You**

Have you ever felt like you were searching for a purpose, for that one thing you were meant to do? That moment when everything finally makes sense, and you realize you're exactly where you're meant to be? I've been on that journey, a long and winding road that led me to the most fulfilling role I could imagine. Today, I can confidently say that I am the luckiest person on earth. I lead a Christian ministry dedicated to guiding women, many of whom struggled with alcohol and drug addiction, towards self-realization, helping them shed the chains of self-doubt, spiritual, emotional, and mental confinement. Together, we embark on a transformative journey to discover their true spiritual identity. My story is a testament to the power of finding one's calling, and it all began with a single step on a path less traveled.

My Heroes Growing Up

My heroes growing up were my two grandmothers and our church pastor. I got to witness these two women work hard, love hard and inspire the people around them. Both of them lived a simple life with few means.

When I was near them, I experienced unconditional love and encouragement. My grandmother would often say, "Sugar, you just gotta be tough". That was her way of saying that sometimes you just got to get tough to get through the hard times.

She had this old cassette tape recorder that she encouraged me to use. I'd walk around her house with the microphone, singing and chatting into it and telling made-up stories. I have always been a natural-born storyteller. I've wanted to tell stories since I can't remember.

My other grandmother would have us over for big dinners and family get-togethers. She was always positive, always encouraging everyone to do good and praise the Lord. The person I loved most at that time in my life was Jesus. I never heard either of my grandmothers ever utter a harsh word against anyone. Both of them were generous with what they had and were always doing things for others. I'd hear them humming gospel music and that encouraged me to join the choir. They were my heroes and I wanted to be like them when I grew up.

Our pastor was like a counselor and a mediator. Whenever there was a problem, you'd go to the pastor. My mom was a good mom. She would sew our clothes and she'd sew little tags into them that said things like, "sewed with love by Janice". She was also a hero of mine and she was a good mama. We didn't always see eye to eye on everything. Daughters and mothers never see eye to eye on everything. But I loved her very much and she loved me.

I think the Lord gave me the gift of gab and the gift of a voice for singing and storytelling. So, with all the confidence in the world, I approached the pastor to discuss my sermon summaries for confirmation class. I'd spent four years in confirmation and I wanted to get more involved in the church. But I was kind of taken aback when he said that girls can't be involved in preaching and those kinds of things. He said girls could clean up the communion silver and also teach Sunday school. The church even provided the lessons to teach. I had the heart and desire to preach like Paul in the New Testament. To be bold like Peter and hopefully one day become a pastor. So this all kind of crushed me on the inside and I really struggled with it. I thought, "How can God, who supposedly loves me and sees me as his own, why can't all these things be for me? How is it that I'm not good enough for that?"

So, all of this kind of set my mind off thinking about who I really was and asking, what was I created to do? It got me questioning a lot of things. This led me on a path of discovering myself and discovering what I should be doing. I'm wired to help others discover themselves too, and to realize that God is there for them and that he loves them and delights in them. No matter what anyone has been through, we are created with a unique purpose, given special gifts from the creator himself to make a difference in the world.

My Big Turning Point

From the moment I was told girls couldn't preach, I began to question everything and fell into self-destructive behaviors. I got into alcohol and drugs and everything in between. I was living on the edge. And I was drowning in self-doubt. If only I could be prettier or richer or more popular. Then one day, I got in a serious automobile wreck. I was drunk and high, totally inebriated. I was trying to fill the void in my soul with anything I could find. I was thrown 35 feet out of the car. I broke my neck in two places, my shoes and purse ended up in the motor of the car, and there was no seat left from where I was sitting. It was an extreme wake-up call.

I was trying to numb out all the voices in my head with every drink. I was tired of trying to be who my mom wanted me to be, who my dad wanted me to be, who my friends wanted me to be; living someone else's life while I tried to live up to everyone else's expectations. I was so confused, I had no idea who I actually was.

"Avoid other people's head trash. Tune out anything that promotes conflict or controversy. This can infect you with a mind virus of cynicism or defeat, and you won't even know it!"

~ Les Brown

It was hard on my family. My brother asked me not to tell anyone that I was his sister. My parents were disappointed and ashamed of me. My friendships fell apart. I couldn't hold a job. My life became totally unmanageable.

The lines of reality got blurry. I was surrounded with lies and dishonesty. I was carrying around this backpack of rocks of labels and shame, and chains and addictions. I fell into a deep dark pit and tried to take my own life. Fortunately, I did a lousy job of it. After a failed marriage and an overdosed suicide attempt, God kind of nudged me into taking stock of myself and my life. I wondered why God would want anything to do with a person like me. I was living in the shadow world of guilt, shame, remorse, lies, and manipulation. I was delirious from confusion about who I was, trying to separate true from false. My family was disappointed and disillusioned with me. My pride and my ego wouldn't allow me to ask for help to climb out of that deep, dark well I was trapped in.

That point, that lowest point, was the beginning of my journey toward self-realization. That was when God's compassion and forgiveness came rushing into my life like a flood. That was the point where I began to understand that I was the beloved daughter of the king. That was the moment when I began to share my newfound revelations with others, to let them know the truth, that God knows them, he sees them. He sees them in the middle of the mess they're in and he loves them anyway. When women like me encounter that love, they begin to realize that their possibilities are endless. I realized that if everyone lived with the realization of their place in the kingdom, the entire world would transform. If we could pass that onto the next generation, and the generations that followed, this world would truly become heaven on earth. I began to dream really big dreams that were inspired from heaven above. Jesus set my soul to dancing.

So, I know that I was created for moments like this to go and encourage and share with others, and sit with ladies in the dirt and change their addictions and say, no girl, you were created for so much more, come on, because God's got a plan for you.

The Stakes Were Life and Death

The accident I was in was extremely traumatic, but it gave me a jolt to catapult my life in another direction. I think if I'd gone on the way I was headed, I wouldn't be here now. I'd be gone. That jolt was the moment when I encountered God in the hospital, with everyone saying, "she needs help". Without that intervention, I would never have made it this far. I would have lost all the friends I still had left. There was just nothing there for me. I would have kept pushing out the boundaries and probably eventually shot dope instead of putting stuff up my nose and down my throat. I would have wound up on the street or in jail probably.

After the wreck, I got involved with the guy I had the wreck with and we got married. It was an escape, a way to get out of the house and away from my parents and all their rules. I thought I was running away from the demons but the demons followed me. Both of us liked to drink and party, filling our souls with all the things the world said would make everything better and get all the voices in my head to shut up. I started to get immune to alcohol. I had to drink more and more just to get a buzz. One drink was one too many and fifty wasn't enough. Our marriage - we only lasted eight months!

So, that's about the time I thought about ending it all. I had to find some way to silence those voices in my head. I don't know if it was a cry for help or whether I was trying to do the world a favor and my parents a favor. I messed up so badly. I was a big disappointment to everybody.

I try not to think about how my life would have been different had I not gotten sober and given my life to Jesus. It would have remained empty and void. I would have continued to be a taker instead of being a giver. I would have continued to cascade down into that well of despair and self-destruction. I kept thinking, this will make me feel better. I'll wake up tomorrow and everything will be better. And it never was. It was always the same and so I'd repeat the cycle and repeat it again. I was a rat on a wheel.

My Internal Struggle

My struggle with the world was a struggle within myself. It was about not believing in myself and chained to this baggage of guilt and shame, remorse and sins, scarlet letters and labels and you name it...

I just dragged all of this around with me. I kept stuffing more and more into the bag. It was hard enough getting from one day to the next, even without this heavy bag of toxic emotional poison. I thought I had gone too far, that I was irredeemable, that there was no hope for me. I'd go to church and sit in the back, hoping no one would see me, hoping no one would recognize me. I sat on the family pew trying to fight through the shame and remorse I felt. I felt everyone's eyes on me, taking pity on my family. I would say things to people just to get them to like me and accept me. I didn't want anyone to talk about me or pity me or my parents. I felt inadequate for so long. I just kept beating myself up.

"Give yourself a break. Stop beating yourself up! Everyone makes mistakes, has setbacks and failures. You don't come into life with a book on how to get it right all the time. Stand up to it and handle it with grace. Because, you can." ~ Les Brown

So, my struggle was, how do I unchain myself from this garbage of emotional baggage? I wondered if there was some switch in my heart that would make it all go away. I needed to get from here to somewhere else. The journey was the road from my heart to my head. My heart craved acceptance and unconditional love, and my head had to learn that those things had to come from my own heart, not anyone else's. It seemed like such a long journey. Even though I was a hot mess, I knew deep down inside that I needed God's love to break free. But all the time, he loved me right where I was. But then there came this moment when I said, "Here's my heart Lord. I'm gonna surrender my life to you. I need your help to tear down this wall between you and me. Here's all the days I've got left in the world. I'm giving it all up to you. You can have it all". And then, day by day, he helped me tear down that wall that I thought was between us, but that was never there in the first place, until one day, we met face to face.

The Road to Redemption

Out there on the road that night, as I was being bounced around like a rock, I saw a bright light. And then everything went dark. When I regained consciousness in the hospital, I remember asking the nurse, "Is this hell?" And later on, in that dim hospital room, with my wrists restrained, and realizing I had even failed at taking myself out, I heard this voice inside saying, "Hey, remember me? I've been here with you the whole time". That's when I knew that somehow, some way, everything was going to be okay.

My road back to sobriety and sanity wasn't easy. I had to earn back everybody's trust. I had to find employment. I had to earn my own trust. Struggling with finances was also an issue, but a bigger issue was just a lack of confidence in myself. I had to believe that God could use me and wanted to use me. How was I going to become a pastor and do God's work without a college degree in theology?

The first time I was asked to speak at an Alcoholics Anonymous (AA) conference, I wasn't even sure what I was going to say. I didn't write a speech or even prepare any notes. I just prayed with a friend and asked God to guide me. And it went pretty well, especially for my first time being up in front of a big group like that. I didn't feel like I belonged up there. I was tooth and nailing it. I was shaking so bad, my insides were a mess. I was sick to my stomach.

But in the midst of that terrifying situation, I knew that God was with me and for me. It gave me hope. I remembered my grandmother's words, "You just gotta be tough". I had faith that God could do for me, what I couldn't do for myself.

I said to myself, "This is it. This is what I'm going to do, what I'm supposed to do. This feels right, sharing my testimony and encouraging others to walk in a way that is different than the way most of the rest of the world walks." After the AA conference, I had many opportunities to share my truth in churches and AA conferences around the world. It was in Peru that I heard God again saying this is what I created for you. This is your purpose.

My confirmation life verse, Psalm 23:1; The Lord is my Shepherd, I shall not want, was from the pastor that told me girls don't preach. In 2010, I saw that same verse in Chincha Peru on the side of a car, written in Spanish. It was like God was saying, "Yes you can, look at you now! This is what I created for you and you shall not want. I gave you the gift to feel and see others in their pain and now you can use it." Since that day, I have woken up every day with a "I get to" mindset. Every day is a gift and I get to!

I wanted to share what I had learned the hard way, that no matter where we are in life, no matter how much we're suffering or how low we've fallen, God is never done with us. We're all a work in progress. You just need to discover whatever it is that makes your soul dance. When Jesus captivates your heart, you get to do the thing that makes your soul dance, and He is the reason you get to do it! The thing that makes your heart go pitter-patter, and use whatever that is to make a difference in the world.

My family was skeptical at first. They didn't understand how I could make this work, how I could make this ministry pay the bills. But by pursuing what I knew was right for me, that experience and that mindset has played an important role in encouraging others to follow their hearts, to follow that inner voice that says, "Come on, let's do this. Walk with me on this path. It may be less traveled, but it's the route that God has laid out for you." My son wanted to write songs. That was his gift. I told him to go ahead, "Get the musical training you need and follow your heart". Songwriting was what he felt God wanted him to do. He followed his dream even when it didn't work the first time around.

No matter what road you take, you're going to encounter roadblocks. The hardship I went through, whether it was the challenges to sobriety or my relationship with God, deepened my relationships with others and helped me walk through my life like it was an adventure. I call it the adventure train! Everything fell in place at first. I met the right people and it seemed like God was opening all the right doors for me. I had a book in progress with a publisher and a podcast ready to launch and my financial affairs were in order. I was traveling all over the country and up into Canada. Then my church came to us and asked us to lead a new missions program. This was the dream job for me.

But then in 2020, my mom had a serious accident that caused a spinal cord injury and she was left quadriplegic. This was during the pandemic and I had to take responsibility for looking after her at home because the hospitals were full and the nursing homes had shut down. The missions program got put on hold during the pandemic because international travel was shut down.We took a loss on our salary and savings remodeling her house to be handicap accessible. It also took a toll on us emotionally and physically. That put the brakes on everything I was doing and I had to surrender all these projects in order to become a full-time caregiver for my mom for almost three years.

I never stopped believing in myself and believing that God had put me into this work to see it through. I got the manuscript completed and sent it to the publisher and now the podcast is getting traction. Now, I've got everything back on track. My dreams were not denied, just delayed.

God gave me a dream for a retreat, so I approached some friends with the idea and we did it. We rented an Airbnb and gathered some women together and it turned out to be this unbelievable, transformational experience for everyone. That made me realize that I just had to keep walking forward and kind of redesign my plans as I went. Now we've done our second retreat and had the ministry filed as a 501c3 charitable organization.

New Ways of Thinking and Being

I had a lot of beliefs and patterns of thinking that held me back originally. Getting rid of these has been like removing a silk scarf from a bramble bush, one thorn at a time. One of the biggest thorns was the thought that I just wasn't good enough. That has probably been my biggest hurdle to overcome. I couldn't conceive of the possibility that God would find me worthy of speaking on his behalf. How or why would he ever want to use someone like me?

"Life has no limitations, except the ones you make."
~ Les Brown

When I was younger, I had a tough time with the lie that girls couldn't carry the message. What I have come to understand is that you don't need to be at a podium and preach in front of a church gathering on Sundays to carry the message. I eventually realized how valuable my life's example was and how I could use the telling of my story to restore my own soul and the souls around me at the same time.

I've also learned to forgive myself and that has led to forgiving others. We have to forgive ourselves first. When we realize our true identity as children of God, our Kingdom identity, we become one with Him. The one who loves us most, the most merciful, and we can accomplish all things in and through Him, while others can tangibly encounter His love through us.

Every morning, I get still and sit with God. I play inspiring music and enter my thoughts into my journal. Sometimes, when things aren't going well, I stop in the middle of the day and start over. I sit still and let my mind settle down. Sometimes I listen to great speakers like Les Brown.

Maybe I'll listen to a sermon. I spend some time each day reading scripture. Over the years, I've embraced the twelve steps program, so sometimes I'll spend some time with that. I embrace forgiveness and self-forgiveness. I spend some time envisioning the things I want to accomplish with my ministry and the different ways I can be used as a channel to uplift and inspire people. I make sure that I not only feed my body with healthy food, I also feed my mind with healthy thoughts and ideas.

My Greatest Rewards

It's difficult to overstate the level of satisfaction I experience when I see the women I work with in my ministry, grow and transform. I watch them break the chains that bind them to addictions and negative patterns of living and thinking and move forward in a positive, healthy direction. I love watching them come to the realization that they are the daughter of the king. They experience a new sense of purpose and adopt a new self-identity. It changes their relationships with their family and friends. These are the moments I live for now, the moments I get to live!

ABOUT

CAUJUAN MAYO

From a young age Caujuan felt like the man of the house, being the oldest of his 6 siblings. Born in New York, the son of a single mother, he grew up in San Diego California, with his 5 brothers, one sister, one cousin, and an aunt. He felt it was his duty to help his mother. This put him in the streets at a young age hustling and living the fast life. It was through gangs and pimping that life eventually caught up with him, landing him in prison, where he served four years for running a high-class escort service.

Upon his release he started a book publishing company, signed three authors, printed over 16 books collectively, produced over five Amazon bestsellers and an audiobook. He commissioned three for Bestselling Author "DUTCH" before discovering the world of Online/Network Marketing in 2012, which truly changed his life, enabling him to earn his first 6 figures in 2014. Since then he has never made a penny less.

Chapter 5
"Using hustle & heart
to change my life"

 Caujuan Mayo

 caujuan

 www.myelitehustle.com

USING HUSTLE AND HEART TO CHANGE MY LIFE

CAUJUAN MAYO

The Roots of an Entrepreneur

I have always wanted to be successful. I was that neighborhood kid looking to sell candy, mudpies, whatever. I could make a business out of anything. So, being a businessman was always in me. And when it's in you, you can lose it all and gain it all back. That's a businessman's superpower. My entrepreneurial drive really birthed me and ultimately saved me in a lot of ways.

Because growing up like I did was rough. When I was born, my dad was heavily rooted in the Five Percent Nation of Islam. So, I was born into a situation where my father could have multiple wives (and with that comes a lot of children). See, children were seen as the greatest asset a man could have, because the more kids a man can populate and educate helps secure the future of the Five Percent Nation.

So, it was already a chaotic household. But on top of that, it was also the crack era. Crack took the world by storm, especially in urban communities. And it created a lot of fatherless households. Because once a person became addicted to crack, it became more important to them than their own family. And unfortunately, my father got involved with crack, and that is when things took a turn for the worse for my family.

My dad got hooked on crack and got involved in living a fast life. He also started becoming abusive with my mother, so the dynamic in my household became really negative and unlivable. One day, my mother had enough. So, she packed us up and moved us to California to start a new life.

A New Beginning But Not a Fresh Start

Even though we had moved as far away as we could get, life wasn't any easier because now my mother was raising seven children alone. But my mother was strong. I don't know how she did it, but she always found a way to make sure we lived in good neighborhoods and had the best clothes. I knew it was a struggle. Life was hard, but I have to hand it to my mom, she didn't make it look that way.

Now, as the oldest male in the household, I knew I needed to step up. My mother is working herself to death to provide for us and as the man of the house, I wanted to help her out. But I was young and no one was going to hire me. So, I didn't have many choices except one: hustling on the streets.

With hustling, I started small, selling clothes or marijuana, anything to provide for my family. But eventually, that evolved into gang-banging. Now, my mom was a good mother. Even my dad, while he was in my life before he took himself out of the picture, was a good role model. So I come from good stock and I had no business being in the streets. But I was a victim of my environment. Like many, I was a victim of my circumstances.

So, it was almost by accident that I started gang-banging. I was hanging out, minding my own business, but I was wearing red (which happened to be my favorite color). But it was also the color of the Bloods. And four or five Crips saw me and told me I had to take the color off or they were going to beat me up.

I happened to have friends around the corner who were Bloods. So, I went and told them what happened. They confronted the Crips for me and they backed down. When I saw them back down that day, I knew I wanted to be a Blood. It was something as simple as that.

Now I know that if my dad was someone who I could have gone to and he would have helped me, things probably would have turned out differently. But I didn't, so instead of wanting to be like my dad, I wanted to be like the Bloods. I wanted to be like the gang members that came to my rescue.

And the gang's influence would have a strong hold on me and influence the choices I made. I would see somebody making serious money on the streets. And suddenly, I would want to have that kind of money too. And I'd try to figure out a way to do it with the choices I had. Even though I was smart enough to know that this was ultimately a dead-end situation. But I looked at it as me using a negative situation to put myself into a positive situation. And I know that sounds backward, but that's what I was doing.

From Husting to Writing

Now, I was always into the hustling side more than the gang-banging side. And I was good at it. I had worked my way from robbing drug dealers to working girls in escort agencies. And I ended up running one of the only black-owned, high-end escort agencies in San Diego. But with that came a huge spotlight that was directed on me. So, here I am still hustling and trying to avoid what comes with that spotlight, but one thing leads to another and I get arrested. And, long story short, I then spent the next 4 years in a penitentiary.

In California, the penitentiary is like a revolving door. Once you go, it's hard to get out. So, being in the penitentiary was a huge wake-up call. It was like the universe knocked me over the head and said, "Get it together, man". For the first time, I could just sit with the choices I was making and look at the actions behind those choices. It gave me time to make the decision to change or keep going. Being inside showed me that this was not a place for me and it made me see I had to change my life.

So, while I was in, I started writing and wrote my first and second book. It felt like a new beginning for me. It gave me the first taste of how success could be built outside of hustling. It also inspired a new aspiration in me to start my own book company when I got out.

Now, down the road, I did start my own book company and published my first book (which is still a 5-star rated book on Amazon). And I kept writing and publishing, eventually signing authors. Now, I have over 20 books on Amazon, with 6 bestsellers to date.

But this was still before my publishing company and it would be my first view of what legitimate success could be like. It was like a light at the end of the tunnel. I realized that I was bigger than the streets. I had more to offer and there was no way I was going back to the penitentiary. I was committed to changing my life for the better.

Because I knew that if I didn't escape a life built by the streets, it was going to take me down. I knew that four years of prison time wasn't anything to sneeze at, but next time zeros would be added to my sentence. And being in prison for 10, 20, 30 years was something I couldn't fathom. I knew that was where I was headed based on what I was doing on the streets.

If You Can Do It, I Can Do It

So, when I had the opportunity to come home on

parole, I took it. The deal was I was let out on parole and if I could stay clean and not cause any problems for 6 months, I would be finished with the system. I kid you not, I locked myself in my room with my computer and I didn't go outside for six months. I wasn't going to do anything that would jeopardize my freedom and make me go back to prison.

And because of that time spent in my room hooked to my computer, I first discovered online trading. Now, I knew how to make a lot of money illegally, but now I wanted to figure out a way to do it legally. So, here I am in my room on the computer and I found someone who has made a significant amount of money in a short amount of time and it was 100% legal. Sign me up.

Online trading opened me up to a different world of people. This was a dynamic circle of free thinkers and entrepreneurs who were chasing money, but legally. And it was through learning about legal ways to make money online that I discovered network marketing.

Now, at that time, I wasn't even sure what online network marketing really was and I definitely didn't know how to do it yet. But people were making a lot of money at it and one thing I knew was that this was something that I could learn how to do and be successful at. See, my motto has always been, "If you can do it, I can do it". I just needed to figure out how. I was certain that, with the right amount of work, I could get that level of success too.

So online marketing became what I wanted to do, but how to start? When I started hustling on the streets, I went all in. So now that network marketing was my focus, I went all in the same way. I was driven by the idea that there was no way I was going back to the streets. I was willing to bet it all on a legit life with network marketing. And while that drive paved the way for me to become very successful my road to success was still not smooth.

The Road to Success Isn't Straight

But success wasn't overnight. Even though I was determined to make it in online marketing, I wasn't making enough money when I started. I was striving, but my gains weren't enough to fund my lifestyle. And then I suffered my greatest personal loss. My mother passed away unexpectedly and it rocked my world. My mother was my rock. She was everything to me.

And when someone passes away unexpectedly I think it can feel worse than when people who have been sick for a long time pass. In the back of your mind, you knew this was coming. But when it just happens out of the blue, it's a gut shot. My mother went into the hospital at 56 years old with a headache and three days later she was gone. She just never came home. She turned 57 in the hospital. It rocked my world. And it sent me to a very dark, very ugly place which took me two years to ultimately come out of.

See, I was trying to make it in online marketing, but I just wasn't making enough money. So, I felt forced into a side hustle. And the best side hustle I knew was working with escorts. Now, I thought I was hustling smart (which is an oxymoron, I know), but one day I took one of the escorts to her date and it was with an undercover officer. I was arrested again.

And I can't even describe how sick from guilt I felt. I just knew I had messed my life up forever. I was terrified of going back to prison and never getting out because my previous case was similar to this one. So, now I'm looking at least 10 years (those zeros, remember?) and my brain just kept thinking "This was dumb, Caujuan. This was so dumb".

But I truly believe my mother was a guardian angel and she had my back. I was bailed out but when I came back to the court, I wasn't on the docket. When I asked about it, I learned that the case was either dismissed or the DA never picked up the case. I'll never really know what happened, but what I do know is that I told myself, "I will never ever be back on these streets again". I knew this was a sign telling me "Look, if you keep it up, this is where you're going to end up."

I was given a pass that day, but I knew that if I kept overplaying my hand, it was like I was throwing rocks at the penitentiary door; eventually, they were going to open that door and let me in.

So, this was a huge wake-up call for me. But it made

me greater, you know? It forced me to find other ways to get ahead and make those other ways work. Which is why I always tell people that sometimes your negative is really a positive. All of our trials are something to make us stronger, you know what I mean? In life, you have to go through it to get to it. And knowing this has really helped me become the person I am today. I feel without those setbacks and those struggles, I would not be as strong as I am right now. So you have to go through the hurt, you have to have the pain. Remember that: You have to go through the pain to get to the gold.

Going Through The Hurt to Get to The Gold

At this point, everything was at stake. I knew if I didn't change my life, I was going to end up in prison doing life or doing some crazy time. What I did have on my side was drive and motivation. Plus, I believed my mother was responsible for my "get out of jail" card so I was determined not to blow it this time.

But while online network marketing showed me there was a different, legal way to make money, I needed to figure out how I was going to make it work for me. So, I looked at my roots and realized I could use my street boss mentality and bring it to the online marketing world to give me an edge.

I began to look at how I could use the skills I used to hustle successfully and leverage it to succeed in the online space. I started by asking myself, "If you were able to get people to pull out their wallets while you were on the streets, how can you not get people to see your vision here with something legit and get them to buy into something that they actually need on a day-to-day basis?"

The approach I took with my online marketing business was taken directly from the lessons I learned on the street. I systematically looked at what worked: people skills, negotiating skills, how to attract the right people, and built my business around what I had learned.

Which is why I'm always seen peacocking. Because I know this attracts clients to me and makes me stand out in the crowd. I started attending networking events, where there are sometimes thousands of people in attendance, but I guarantee you are always able to pick me out of the crowd. This is all done by design.

A pivotal point in my success came when I took the time to build my brand. I focused on making my brand become a household name and the strategy I used was to put my brand in everybody's face. I wanted to make sure every marketer, networker and everybody in the world aspiring to be one knew about Caujuan Mayo.

See, if you ask a kid if they're hungry and if they want a burger. 9 times out of 10 they'll say yes. And if you ask them where they want to go, 10 times out of 10, they're going to say McDonalds. Every kid in America and around the world knows the Golden Arches. That is the kind of branding I knew I had to do. In a way, I aspired to be a kind of rockstar in the marketing world because I knew that by growing my visibility it would also grow my net worth.

And since that pivotal moment, it's just been up, up, up ever since. My life changed dramatically in 2017 when I made $10,000 in a month online. And then $10k/month became my usual. That really changed the trajectory of everything. I suddenly got the attention of the world and the masses.

Knowing When to Pivot

Now, even though I was making money with network marketing, I felt at the mercy of the companies I worked with. One month I was on top of the leaderboard and the next month, I'd find myself in the middle with the same level of work output. That's when I realized that the best way to secure the bag was to create the bag. I wasn't just looking for a paycheck. What I wanted was to build a dynasty.

So, I reinvented myself again and became an entrepreneur. I started coming up with my own companies and creating my own softwares. I wanted to put myself in a position where I'm not going to fire myself. And since I don't have to worry about pleasing anyone but myself, I can focus on securing the bag.

It doesn't matter what niche you're in, whether it's

network marketing, online marketing, MLM, or even traditional business, this is a lesson all entrepreneurs need to know. Once we start making money, the biggest mistake we make is that we then spend the money. We've worked hard so we want our lifestyle to reflect that.

But if you spend thousands of dollars on stuff and jewelry, at the very least you have to make thousands. So, when I say "secure the bag", I mean that in order for me to spend thousands, I have to make tens of thousands. In order for me to spend hundreds of thousands, I have to make millions. That's always been my mentality. And I think it's one that most entrepreneurs get wrong once they start making money and getting successful.

The Entrepreneur's Legacy

But when you're an entrepreneur, it opens up so many more doors and so many more opportunities. With network marketing, people are making money off of you. But as an entrepreneur, everything I was doing to promote their businesses, I was now doing for my own and I got to keep 100% of the profit.

And once I made that shift, it was a game changer. Now I'm not just an affiliate, but I'm actually a business owner. I own several businesses, from software to book publishing. And since I've built such a visible brand, more and more people reach out to me because they're trying to get into business for themselves.

So, I've also created a platform where people can learn everything that I know and everything that I've done to become successful. They can use my lessons to learn to be successful themselves. Because I've realized that our success is all connected. The more people that I help get to where they're trying to go in life, the more they want to see me get to where I want to go.

And that's the reason why I stay true to myself because I want to motivate the person that looks like me. I want to motivate that person who doesn't want to put on the stuffy suit and be someone they're not. They don't have to do all that. I show them they can be themselves and succeed. I show them they can live through the roughest things life can throw at them and they can still turn their lives around. One of my favorite things about network marketing is that "You can be from Yale or jail, and still be successful here".

I'm proof of that. So, I started a platform to help other people like me also become successful. I want them to have a place that shows them it doesn't matter if they are a convicted felon, or have been to prison before. It doesn't matter if some people clench their purses when they walk by. None of these things matter anymore. I teach them they can take the bull by the horns. Because I've learned I control my life. I control my outcome. I control my reality. And I ultimately control my success.

And so can you.

GERALD J. LEONARD

Gerald offers a unique productivity approach to accomplishing more every day. Gerald J. Leonard PMP, PfMP, and a C-IQ Coach is the publishing editor, CEO, and founder of the Leonard Productivity Intelligence Institute, as well as the CEO of Turnberry Premiere, a strategic project portfolio management and IT governance firm based in Washington, DC.

Gerald is also an author, TEDx speaker, management guru, and, importantly, a bass player. He brings all these traits and skills into his presentations and interviews.

Gerald is the host of the Syndicated podcast Productivity Smarts and the author of A Symphony of Choices (A Business Parable), Culture Is The Bass, and Workplace Jazz.

Chapter 6
"Finding the beat in adversity:
a story of music, mind & mastery"

 Gerald Leonard Pfmp

 geraldjleonard

 www.geraldjleonard.com

FINDING THE BEAT IN ADVERSITY:
A STORY OF MUSIC, MIND, AND MASTERY

GERALD J. LEONARD

My parents didn't just raise me and my siblings, they protected our hearts and minds. I was the youngest of six in the vibrant era of the '60s, wrapped in a cocoon of love and security so firm that the storms of racial tension brewing outside barely registered as a whisper. This tells you just how well my parents cared for us. They gave us complete security and ensured that my siblings and I grew up in a home where the only battles were over who got the last slice of pie.

Let me take you back to when I was little. I'm around 7, my fingers reluctantly dancing across piano keys. I would play, but I didn't like it that much. It wasn't the melody of my heart, though, and I would continue to take lessons for years.

Now, the guitar my sister owned? That was more my speed. By age ten, I was stealing her guitar, strumming strings that resonated with my soul. Eventually, she'd find me, and I'd give it back until she let me have it one day. And I can't explain how much I loved that little red guitar. Can you remember that first spark of passion igniting within you? That's what music and that guitar did for me.

Every day, I'd listen to the radio and practice, tirelessly decoding the secret language of music, note by note. The radio wasn't just a machine; it was my teacher, my muse. But I wanted more.

Eventually, I joined a band with some friends who were dreamers like myself, but they already had an excellent guitar player, which led me to a new musical discovery —the bass guitar.

Around that same time, in Lakeland, Florida, they created the Lakeland Civic Center, where I witnessed musical greats like Earth, Wind and Fire, Ohio Players, and Bootsy Collins. I saw all of these amazing musicians up close and personal. And I tell you what, their music wasn't just heard; it was felt, a tangible force that fueled my midnight practice sessions. After one of those concerts, I would go home and practice my bass until 3 a.m.

My childhood was a serene melody, a privilege I owe to my parents' unwavering support. But that doesn't mean everything was handed to me. I had to learn to pay for things outside of necessities, so I didn't stay a stranger to hard work. Whether mowing lawns or completing chores, every cent I earned was a note in the composition of my character. Being a musician and working for my own money taught me the value of hard work and investment in my craft.

High school brought a crescendo of commitment to my music. I kept playing, of course, because I wanted to continue to grow in my ability to perform. However, my focus on music overshadowed my academic performance, and I didn't graduate with enough credits or a good enough GPA to get into college.

But, despite an academic performance that wasn't quite ovation-worthy in the classroom, I did get into the Berklee College of Music for a certification program. And I spent a summer after graduation in Illinois with my brother and his wife, in what was supposed to be a prelude to my college life in Boston. But little did I know that fate had a different score in mind.

I was staying with them and all set to leave for college in the fall when I met a gentleman named Lamont Parson. Lamont was a jazz guitar player, and we started playing music together. He had a son in college and told me about his school, Central State University. He then shared that he was friends with someone in the music department and that I should check it out.

So, I auditioned at CSU two months before I was to leave for Berklee. I got into the marching band there and received a full scholarship, a turning point in my life. That opportunity made me realize that just as I was passionate about music, I needed to develop that same passion for my academics.

And so I was determined to do just that. Now, I don't want to make out that it was all sweet melodies. The risk of failure loomed over me like a dark cloud

- threatening to send me back to Florida if I failed. Destined to work in construction alongside my father in the hot sun—And so I had to work my butt off to get good at academics. But I think my experience of working to learn the guitar and all the hours of practice needed to master the instrument laid a solid foundation for me to do just that.

Not only could I play music and enjoy myself, but I did the work to keep my grades up and maintain my full scholarship. I ended up finishing four years there and then getting a full scholarship to Cincinnati Conservatory, where I was to do my master's in classical double bass.

Having all my hard work pay off was incredible, but that experience also opened my eyes to additional lessons. Learning how to network, a skill as crucial as any scale or arpeggio, would open doors I never knew existed. First, my meeting with Lamont Parson introduced me to Dr. Omoku at CSU, who started my version of sixth-degree separation that ultimately paved the way for the opportunities that shaped my future.

So, these early lessons were ones I've never forgotten and used in my entire career and life. I've never forgotten to practice my instrument (or craft), join a band (immerse yourself in a community of like-minded individuals), seek a mentor or coach, and network with heart and purpose. Do these things, and you will find that life moves from dissonance to harmony.

A Symphony of Resilience

After getting my master's degree, I moved to New York and did some ministry work for the next 7-8 years. But it wasn't long before music sounded its siren song, and I realized what I wanted to be was a musician.

But now my life includes a wife and children. And the thought of going on the road, being an absentee father, was not an option. I remember how my dad was always there for me, so I was determined to find a way to have music and augment my career locally so I could be there for my kids.

So, I began learning about computers and became an IT consultant. I would play concerts and recitals while working as a consultant. And in doing so, I began to see a synergy between music and business that I would leverage for over a decade.

Getting Better Without Getting Bitter

So, 18 years have passed, and I have moved my family to Maryland. I'm now heavily into consulting and playing music at the church, recitals, and different venues around the area. But as our children grew older, things became more complex in my marriage. I was starting to feel like I was walking on shaky ground. And then, one day, as I took a shower to prepare for a workshop, life would knock me down.

Suddenly, I couldn't tell up from down. I was rushed to the emergency room, where I ended up spending a day and a half before I would receive a diagnosis that would change everything. I had a significant event with vertigo, I had lost 86% of hearing capability in my right ear, and I was now unable to balance myself.

Now, they couldn't explain why it happened. To get released, I needed to show them that I could use a walker to scoot down the hall. It took all my energy to do that, but I did and was released. But I had essentially lost my entire ability to walk on my own. I was now disabled.

I can't describe how devastating it was to come home. I lay in bed for a week because it felt like someone had hit me in the head with a baseball bat. The vertigo made me feel like I was midship in the middle of the ocean. And that's when my mind would start spinning, thinking, "Is this the rest of my life?" I didn't allow myself to go to a dark place with my thoughts, but when I asked myself that, I realized I needed to figure out how to get out of that bed. I needed to find a way to get back on my feet.

If you've ever found yourself in the middle of a storm, where every lightning strike feels like a direct hit to your life, then you know how I felt. Just think about it: a life you've built for nearly three decades crumbles before you. Your health, your marriage, your home—everything you've held dear is suddenly on the line. This was my reality. I knew I had to dance with change or be trampled by it.

And professionally, this was not the time to give up either. See, in 6 weeks, I was to give a TEDx talk titled "What If Practice Is the Performance," where I would talk about the neuroscience of music.

And so, as soon as I could get up alone, I went to my office and grabbed my bass. I started playing every day, and music became part of my therapy.

Yes, it was hard. My recovery felt like I was an NFL football player recovering from a major hit with collateral body damage. Each step was hard won. I would listen to music and cry because I was in such bad shape. But I never gave up. I knew I had no choice if I wanted to get better. So, my recovery was rooted in a decision to move forward no matter what.

Each day, I would walk a little further and play my bass, each note a defiant march against my condition. Within three weeks of playing music and walking daily, I could walk into my doctor's office unassisted. Three weeks later, I stepped on stage and delivered my TEDx talk. My talk on the neuroscience of music was no longer just a topic but a lived experience. Through the gift of music, I found my footing again.

But even though I was healing from the physical challenges, my personal life continued to suffer. After a 28-year marriage, my wife and I decided to divorce. The pain over losing that relationship and relinquishing my home, my sanctuary, and all the memories it held rivaled physical pain. Yes, I was scared. But lying down and giving up? That wasn't my tune. I had to move forward to be better.

When the Only Way is Forward

During this time, my children, now adults, became my support. Vertigo had forced me to step back from my role as their ever-present father, and they had to mature swiftly, facing unscripted trials. But together, we found our rhythm again.

Looking back, I realize that if I had chosen to be bitter rather than to get better, I might still be confined to a bed, dependent on a walker, trapped in an unsupportive marriage. Instead, I have a successful consulting business and am a recognized artist and musician. I'm a keynote speaker for major corporations, national associations, and conferences. I am genuinely a composition of my choices.

Without the decision to embrace change, to move with life's unpredictability, my narrative could have been a song of struggle marred by cognitive and health issues. But those choices, those pivotal moments of choosing to triumph over adversity rather than drown in despair, radically altered the course of my life.

Les says, "When life knocks you down, try to land on your back. Because if you can look up, you can get up. Let your reason get you back up."

Dancing with Change: A Rebirth

I was now at a place where I needed to rebuild my life as well as fully recover my health. Yes, I was walking, but I still wasn't 100%. So, I leaned into the lessons that made me a great musician.

I dove headfirst into the world of neuroscience and productivity, seeking out coaches and brain gyms, anything that could help me understand and combat the resistance I was facing. I educated myself about how the brain recovers from injury, and I started to push back against the limitations I felt both inside and out.

Money was tight. I had become the sole breadwinner, juggling two homes—one in Maryland, a new start in Alabama, and mounting medical debts. My friends did what they could, but no one truly grasped the gravity of my situation. It was a dramatic shift in my life that left me feeling somewhat isolated in my journey.

But let me tell you, when I underwent a brain scan and saw the physical impact of a negative relationship on my brain; it was a wakeup call. I decided then and there to work on myself. I read everything I could get my hands on, attended therapy, and sought the support I needed.

I learned the power of letting go, moving on, and delving back into consulting while maintaining my client base. It was time to grow, expand my consciousness, and discover what I didn't know.

Neuroscience, meditation, yoga, qigong, and energy management became my classroom for growth.

It was my self-limiting beliefs that were holding me back. I'm sure you've had them too: I wasn't good enough, smart enough, couldn't make enough money. These beliefs held me back, but I hadn't realized it until now.

Through various coaches, I learned to challenge these beliefs to remove them from my unconscious and subconscious mind. These techniques radically transformed my life.

I got certified in the neuroscience of Conversational Intelligence under Judith Glaser before her passing and worked with Dr. Paul Sheele, and Jack Canfield. I learned about the conscious and non-conscious mind, yoga, and meditation. Then, a friend introduced me to a powerful method to manifest goals—writing them out by hand daily. I started this practice in February 2020, visualizing and meditating on my goals daily. The transformation was nothing short of miraculous.

By November 2020, a large company invested in my business, resolving my financial challenges and back taxes. That year, I remarried, bought a new home, grew my company, and authored two more books. And now, I'm working on a fourth.

Writing my goals every day, practicing what I preach, and having a supportive team, mentors, and coaches—this transformed my life. It's not just about setting goals; it's about the daily discipline, the belief in yourself, and the harmony of support that can turn your life's composition into a masterpiece.

The Rich Tapestry: Weaving a Life of Triumph

When I look back, the tapestry of my life is far richer and more colorful than I ever imagined it could be. I've written three books, with two published by major publishers. I've stood on stage as a keynote speaker, earning five-figure salaries and five-figure contract payments for speaking. My companies? They're thriving, sailing well into the high seven-figure mark.

I'm not just talking numbers here; I'm talking about a life enriched with experiences and providing for my new wife, whisking her away to the Cayman Islands, Hawaii, and London. Sometimes, I feel like I'm living in a canoe, gently floating down the river of life, going with the stream, embracing the flow of prosperity and joy.

But let me tell you, this doesn't come without daily practice. I still write out my goals and affirmations every day. I maintain a serene mind through yoga and meditation and de-stress regularly. This daily ritual discipline is the paddle that keeps my canoe on course.

And with this success comes the ability to give more to my family, to help my mother-in-law, and to support my church. There was a time when I doubted I'd ever reach this point, but here I am, not just surviving but thriving, giving back in ways I once thought impossible.

You know, it's pretty remarkable. As I get older, I feel younger. Why? Because I'm living my best life. We've found excellent doctors for my previous health issues, and my well-being has improved dramatically. I sleep better and manage my weight effectively, and I know none of this would have happened if I hadn't decided to fight through my darkest times, to emerge unscathed but as a better person.

Staying grounded is key. With success, I knew I had to stay humble and stay hungry. I have to focus on where I'm going—not just on what I've achieved, but on what's still to come.

Understanding the neuroscience of success aligning your mental, emotional, and heart and brain energy into a coherent state is crucial. It creates an energy field that transforms you into someone who will attract your desired life and lifestyle. It's been an incredible journey that began through pain but continued through learning and growth.

Each day, I write down what I'm grateful for, taking time to appreciate the good in my life. I practice Heart-math, spending 5 to 10 minutes daily on deep breathing, allowing my heart and brain to synchronize, becoming more coherent, and healing my body.

Now, I have the privilege of teaching others how to manifest the life they want, align their goals, and destress their bodies. Whether through podcasts, my newsletter, radio and television interviews, or keynote speeches, I share the lessons I've learned about mindfulness and personal growth.

And here's what I want you to understand: You don't have to go through a dramatic or catastrophic event to learn these lessons. While adversity can be an influential teacher, it's not a prerequisite for growth. Start where you are, with what you have, and you'll be amazed at how far you can go.

ABOUT

SABRINA GRAHAM

Sabrina Graham is a multi-business owner with a dream to build a legacy to keep families together. She has a career as a Project Manager with over 10 years of experience. She's also a real estate investor and volunteers with Girl Scouts as a troop leader for over five years now.

In August of 2023, she started a new business to educate people on the perks of having excellent credit, based on her personal experience of reaching a perfect FICO 8 credit score multiple times. Sabrina is originally from Florida but currently resides in Texas with her husband and daughter.

Chapter 7
"A dreamer's tapestry: building homes & mastering credit"

 Mrs. Perfect Credit

 mrs.perfectcredit

 www.excel-in-credit.ueniweb.com

CHAPTER VII

A Dreamer's Tapestry: Building Homes and Mastering Credit

Sabrina Graham

Growing up as the youngest of three, life was like a vibrant tapestry woven with the wisdom, love, and laughter of a family. My mother and father were my earliest teachers for the game of life. We lived under one small but mighty roof, where my parents stood as pillars of strength, generosity, and growth. With my mom's prudent budgeting and my dad's wise investment mindset gave them a bigger vision of purchasing the apartment next door as their future investment. They were my heroes, shaping my world with every act of kindness, every sacrifice they made to fulfill not just our needs but even the wants that twinkled in our youthful eyes.

Think about the first time you realized someone was your hero. Maybe it was a parent, a teacher, or a friend. For me, it was seeing my parents' faces light up with pride at our smallest achievements, observing my parents stretch a dollar, and soothing our worries about expenses with their financial wisdom. They gave from the heart, whether it was a second-hand bicycle restored to look new or a brand-new game that lit up our evenings. Their love was the blueprint for my own dreams of financial independence and giving back.

103

Another hero of mine, the one and only Oprah, danced across our television screen with a grace that rivaled the stars. Her generosity on her show was like watching the magic unfold, a kind of giving that reached through the screen and whispered, "You can be this, too." And so, a seed was planted deep within me. A dream to grow up and become a giver, to spread joy and hope as she did.

But even heroes face trials, and my journey was no different. Can you remember a time when you faced something really tough? I had to find my voice, both literally and figuratively, as speech didn't come easy to me. Many days were spent away from school, in the company of therapists who patiently untangled the knots in my words. And then, there was the day the car came rushing towards me—a day that fractured more than just my leg. Yet, from that wreckage, I rose to run faster than ever before, to become a track star who sprinted past doubt and fear.

The teasing at school, the nicknames, the taunts— they were like stones on my path. But I learned to step over them, to use them to build my resolve. It's in the games I played as a child, like Monopoly and the Game of Life, where I found a reflection of my ambitions. Houses and hotels weren't just pieces on a board; they were symbols of a future I yearned to build—a future with a home for everyone I loved.

Did you know that the things we deeply desire can

become the compass that guides our lives? For me, that compass pointed towards creating a better future for my family. Dreaming of big homes with ample space and personal bathrooms was more than a child's fantasy; it represented a promise of comfort and a token of gratitude for the love that had been bestowed upon me.

In the pursuit of these dreams, there was much at stake. You might remember a feeling of wanting to avoid regrets. That was a driving force for me. I lived with a sense of urgency, knowing that time is a treasure that can't be reclaimed. I didn't want to look back and wish for more time, opportunities, and abundance in my life. When my father passed before I could build his dream home, I found solace in the memory of a suite by the lake, a temporary palace where he was king, if only for a moment.

I've since built another house, though not the dream home yet, it stands tall with two stories of triumph with a balcony to sit on to glance at a beautiful lake with different size boats passing by. In every corner, I see the possibility of what's to come, a reminder that "all things work together for the good." My faith assures me that I am walking the path meant for me, fulfilling a purpose that is uniquely mine, even if it takes forms I never expected.

The Climb: Rising Above Roadblocks to Reach the Stars

Life, much like a construction project, is full of unexpected roadblocks. I remember how my shyness was like a bubble, a safe sphere that kept the world at bay. "How do you push past your comfort zone?" is a question I often reflect on. For me, it was a gradual process of stepping out, speaking up, and connecting with others. It was necessary for growth, like a seed pushing through the soil towards the sun.

As a black woman, I grappled with confidence, specifically in my financial capabilities, with understanding my worth in a field dominated by men. It wasn't just about knowing—it was about believing. "Did you know that knowledge could only take you so far without belief?" It's a lesson I learned as I delved into real estate investing and development, absorbing knowledge like a sponge. Yet, what held me back was not a lack of understanding, but a fear of failure, a ghost from past attempts that didn't pan out as I'd hoped.

Failure, as I've come to know it, is a poignant teacher. Have you ever felt the sting of a setback? It's a feeling I'm all too familiar with, like the real estate flip that fell through, leaving us with a financial wound. It was during these moments that I leaned heavily on my faith, reminding myself that money is a resource given and taken by God and that each loss was a lesson in disguise.

Yet, failure is not a solitary experience. Think about how your challenges affect those around you. My husband, my rock, feels the ripples of my setbacks, yet his unwavering support is a testament to the strength of our bond. My daughter, still young, may not fully grasp the weight of these moments, but I strive to explain, to share the purpose behind our sacrifices. It's for her future, to be able to take trips to Europe and Japan, for the experiences that money enables, that we work and sometimes stumble along this path.

But within me burned a relentless drive, a refusal to see failure as a dead end. It took time to recognize that my voice mattered. That behind the exterior, my heart and wisdom were what truly spoke volumes. Embracing my identity, my race, and my gender became a daily conquest—one that I continue to fight with growing pride and confidence.

Leading in fields where my culture was seldom seen at the helm added layers to the climb. It was a battle of perception, of learning to stand tall in my skin, to embrace my identity with pride, and let my heart and wisdom shine through. Once people saw beyond the exterior, they connected with the essence of my message, and that became my focus. Allowing me to continue to look up and reach for the stars.

Blueprints for Change: Embracing a New Direction

There comes a time in every dreamer's path when the

road forks and a choice must be made. For me, that moment came after years of chasing the elusive goal of flipping houses. What would you do if the dream you chased seemed to slip through your fingers? The answer lay not in the persistence of pursuit but in the courage to embrace a new direction.

I had been so fixated on one way to achieve my goals that I almost missed the signs pointing me elsewhere. Then, like a beacon, the land we had purchased, which sat patiently waiting, came back into focus. Have you ever had a moment of clarity that changed everything? That's what happened to me. It was as if the land itself was inviting me to walk its expanse, to envision the possibilities that lay dormant in its rich soil.

During this time of reflection, I recalled the words of the First Lady, Michelle Obama, who spoke to our Girl Scouts about the power of pivoting. Her message resonated with me deeply, confirming that it was time to turn my attention from flipping homes to purchasing land. This pivot was not a step back, but a leap forward into a realm that felt surprisingly right. It was in the open fields, with the wind whispering through the grass, that I found a love for new construction and the seeds of my future endeavors.

Becoming Your Own Yes: The Ultimate Freedom By Mastering Credit

Financial approvals, loans, and investments posed their own hurdles. Hearing 'no' when trying to invest in my future was disheartening, but it taught me to become my own 'yes.' I polished my credit score to excellence, turning it from a barrier into a bridge. And as for self-sabotage, that insidious habit of starting strong but faltering before the finish line, it was a pattern I sought to break. "What are you doing to break free from self-sabotage?" is a question I posed to myself as I faced my fears head-on. With this time not just stopping at excellent credit, but gaining the rare perfect credit score.

Having excellent credit isn't just about financial transactions; it's a statement of independence and self-empowerment. It means being able to invest in opportunities that once seemed out of reach, being able to build wealth, being able to leave a legacy and an inheritance, and being able to step into the role of a giver.

How do you plan to shape the future? My newfound insights into credit and financial stability have become a beacon for my community. By championing the message that perfect credit is attainable for anyone, I'm dismantling stereotypes and empowering others to take control of their financial destinies. The ripple effect of my success is already evident as I watch my family and others around me strive for home ownership and financial literacy.

Achieving perfect credit granted me the ultimate freedom—the power to be my own 'yes.' No longer at the mercy of financial institutions, I could make bold moves and investments with confidence. It's a liberating feeling that I wish for everyone, the ability to pursue opportunities without the constraints of poor credit holding you back.

For me, my journey doesn't end with personal success; it's about creating a collective future where families thrive together. My dream is to build communities that foster unity and support. It's not just about the houses I build or the credit scores I help improve—it's about the families that grow stronger within those homes, the marriages that flourish, and the children who will inherit a world of possibilities.

Guiding Lights: From Shadows to Spotlights

It wasn't until I graduated from a program led by Serita Jakes, based on T.D. Jakes' book "God's Leading Ladies: Out of the Shadows and into the Light," that I realized I had been in hiding and it was time to emerge. Through this program, I completed my first speaking engagement and was invited back the following year to speak again. My voice and message were validated and heard, weaving another thread of confidence into the tapestry of my journey.

Building a house on the first lot we owned was another testament to this shift. The doors that once seemed shut now swung open, welcoming me to a path that was always meant for me. "Think about a door that's always been open to you," I'd share with others. Sometimes the opportunity we seek is not behind a locked door but through one that's been waiting for us to walk through all along.

With this realization, my approach to real estate transformed. I learned that the art of building homes was not just about the physical structure but about laying down roots for families, for communities. It was a calling that went beyond the transactional—it was about creating spaces where memories could be made and legacies established.

The journey to this point was not without its financial pressures. A balloon loan on our first mortgage was like a ticking time bomb, a constant reminder of what could be lost. Which would you rather be: stressed about the future or confident in your ability to navigate it? The stress propelled me to master the intricacies of credit, to ensure such a threat would never loom over my family again. It was a journey from ignorance to enlightenment, from fear to control.

As my understanding deepened, so did my credit score, until it shone with the luster of perfection. This was not just a personal victory; it was a beacon for others, a demonstration that with the right knowledge and determination, anyone could achieve financial stability. It was about breaking stereotypes and empowering not just myself but my entire community to dream bigger, to aim higher.

Laying the Keystone: From Vision to Reality

The true measure of success is not only in the heights one reaches but in the depths from which one has come. Think about how far you've come from where you started. It wasn't just a house; it was a milestone, a symbol that dreams, no matter how ambitious, have the power to cross the distance between imagination and reality.

Meeting Janice Bryant Howroyd, a black woman who had turned her passion into billions, was like looking into a mirror that reflected not what was, but what could be. Her success was not merely in the numbers but in the impact she had on people's lives, on the community, on the world. "Did you know that success is more than just making money?" It's about making a difference, and that was the kind of success I yearned for—a legacy of helping families thrive together.

In my journey, I learned that financial understanding was the bedrock upon which such dreams could be built. Money, often a taboo subject, was a vital tool—a means to an end. It was about transcending the stereotype that financial literacy was beyond our grasp. By achieving a perfect credit score myself, I became a living example that it was possible, and more importantly, I could show others the way.

Education was the key. How do you pass on what you've learned to the next generation? By teaching. By empowering not just oneself but enabling others to stand on their own. It's one thing to give a man a fish, another to teach him to fish, and yet another to teach him to teach fishing. That's how legacies are built, how cycles of limitation are broken.

By empowering others about credit and financial literacy, I'm laying the groundwork for generational wealth and stability. Ownership isn't just about having a deed to a piece of property; it's about claiming your place in the world and having the power to shape your destiny.

My sister and brother began to see the transformation, the shift from dreaming to doing. They too wanted to improve their scores, to walk the path of homeownership, to secure their financial futures. The movement was no longer just about me; it was about us, about lifting each other up, about becoming a collective 'yes' to our aspirations.

As I look back on the path I've traveled, from the speech therapy sessions that tried to box in my voice, to standing tall in my identity, leading and teaching, I see a story of victory. Not just my victory, but one I share with every person who has been a part of my journey. Can you see how your story is part of a bigger picture? It's a tapestry we weave together, each thread essential, each color vibrant.

Constructing Success: The Joy of New Beginnings

The tapestry of my life, interwoven with the threads of trials and triumphs, serves as a testament to my belief in God. How do you find strength when you're standing in the middle of a storm? For me, it was always about looking up and trusting that I am guided, and that every step, every stumble, is part of God's plan for my life.

With my credit score as my foundation, I've become a dream builder, not just for myself, but for those around me. The success I've garnered in real estate and finance is not just a personal triumph; it's a beacon for others to follow. My story is a testament that with determination, education, and the right mindset, building dreams is not just possible—it's inevitable.

The trips to Europe and Japan aren't just vacations; they're educational experiences, they're investments in my daughter's future—a future I am crafting with every lesson I learn, every setback I overcome. What investments are you making in the future you desire? It's a question that drives me, that propels me forward with the knowledge that each effort, each sacrifice, is for a purpose greater than myself.

The ability to give back—to my family, to my community, to those in need—is the true reward of my journey. It's a joy that transcends material possessions, one that comes from seeing the lives of others improved because I was able to lend a helping hand.

As a black woman, an entrepreneur, a mother, a wife each role I play comes with its own set of challenges, but also its own unique rewards. I've learned to wear my identity as a badge of honor, to use my voice to inspire and lead, to showcase that beauty and strength come in all shades and stories. How do you embrace the roles you play in life? By owning them, by using them as platforms to elevate not only oneself but also those who look to you for guidance, for inspiration.

My journey is far from over, but the chapters already written are filled with lessons of resilience, of grace, of unwavering determination. I've built more than just a house; I've begun constructing a home for dreams—a home where hopes are not just whispered wishes but shouts of certainty.

And as I stand here today, I know that my story is not mine alone. It belongs to every person who has dared to dream, to every soul that has faced adversity and risen stronger. "Think about your own story, your own journey," I'd invite you to consider. We are all builders in this life, crafting our destinies one brick, one choice, one dream at a time.

ABOUT

JULIE DUNCAN

Over thirty years Julie Duncan has worked to inspire, influence, and provide change for people of all age groups and backgrounds.

Her work in child protective services, mental health, drug and alcohol, school counseling, education, insurance and health and wellness all play a pivotal role in her Life Coaching. Empowering women is now her pride and joy.

Julie's passion is working with clients to follow through on their goals and fulfill their potential. She finds nothing more gratifying than working side by side with her clients, watching them transform into the person that they have desperately been looking for most of their life.

As a Certified Master Life Coach, Julie provides a coaching blueprint based upon her clients' goals. Empowering Life Coaching is a results-driven program.

Chapter 8
"Coming full square"

🅕 Empowering Life Coaching & Consulting, LLC

🅞 empowering_lifecoaching

🌐 www.julieduncancoaching.com

COMING FULL SQUARE

JULIE DUNCAN

E ach of us is born in a box, a square of sorts. My box began growing up in Warren, a rural town in Northwestern Pennsylvania. Hayfields ran the length of long windy roads, marking country living, while simple folk went about their day. Some of my fondest memories include riding bikes with my friends, meeting at the local store for penny candy, and playing kick the can at dusk. Those neighborhood friends provided me with a sense of community and belonging; a feeling all children long for during their young lives.

In high school, I met people who would become lifelong friends and have an even greater impact on my life. Some of those include Susan, Beth, Theresa, Lisa, Terri, Brenda, Denise, and Holly. These were the influencers of my life.

Their influence and character were never more evident than when my brother, Doug, was killed in a triple fatality car accident during my senior year of high school. It was 1980 and my friends carried me through the most painful time of my life. As the news spread, one by one, they came to my home to ease my pain, if only for a minute.

A few days after Doug's burial some of them piled

into a car and drove to my house on a cold, snowy night. Any diversion from my newfound reality was always welcome. I had lived in profound grief since the officer stood at our front door and announced the news that my brother had died. I remember walking outside together; the moonlight, the pristine blanket of snow covering the ground, and falling snowflakes created a sense of magic. I didn't want the night to end. It signified the love best friends carry for each other. I was a normal teenager, at least for a few hours. Although it would take time to mend my heart from the loss of my brother, my friends played a key role in my healing.

What I learned from my friends is that life goes on and that "Love is often disguised as Friendship."

My friends steered me through the process of what I was going to do with my life after high school. They all had plans post graduation. I had not taken action and was feeling left behind, even though I hadn't yet graduated. FOMO (Fear of Missing Out) is very real! I was deeply grief-stricken, while determined to fulfill a dream my brother could no longer pursue. He was a proud U.S. Air Force serviceman when he died. He planned to enroll in college. I wanted to honor him by going to college, little did I know I would be honoring myself.

A Life-Defining Moment

My life-defining moment was the day I sat across the desk of my high school guidance counselor, Mr. King. The room looked brighter than usual as the sun peered through the floor-to-ceiling windows. There was a distinctive smell in his office of academia spewing through the dust-covered books on his shelf.

It was the spring of my senior year, and I was there to pick up my application to Edinboro University where my best friend and I were going to embark upon the next stage of our lives. Although I loved my small rural town, I had my sights on so much more. I had dreamt of a college degree since I was a little girl. I was eager to earn my degree and explore the world.

Little did I know my dreams and aspirations would come crashing down with a few words uttered by Mr. King, "You are not college material." So profound was this moment forty years ago that as I type this now, I still become outraged at his one-dimensional thinking.

"You should become a manager at Burger King," said Mr. King, which left me speechless.

I don't remember much after those words spewed out of his mouth and was grateful it was the end of the day. I left school and didn't talk to anyone. I just wanted to get home. I felt utterly broken. My mind was hyperfocused on Mr King's cruel words. It's amazing how someone's words can pierce one's soul.

As I took the time to process this life-defining

moment, ironically Mr. King wasn't entirely wrong. Skipping classes, partying with my friends, and doing just enough in high school to get by didn't make for a stellar college application.

He was, however, wrong about a few things. At the age of seventeen, I refused to allow this to break me. I had just survived burying my brother and I was lucky enough to have both a role model and a grandmother, named Genevieve. She always had words of wisdom during times of distress. I remember my beloved grandmother telling me the story of sitting on a train for three to four hours traveling to Penn State College, now Penn State University, in the 1930s to earn her teaching degree.

She understood the power of education because her mother died when she was three years old, leaving her father, a rural farmer, with the responsibility of raising seven children on his own. From a young age, I knew I would follow in her footsteps, clearly in a different direction than Mr. King had in mind for me.

"Everyone should have a Genevieve in their life."

The Voices

Due to my grandmother's guidance and powerful words, I took a deep breath, walked into the guidance office, and demanded an application for Edinboro University. The secretary happily handed me the application and said, "I know you will do great."

Against all odds, I meticulously filled out the college application, mailed it to the Admissions department, and waited for the decision that would make or break the rest of my life.

Six weeks after submitting my application, I was working at Burger King when my mother busted through the front door waiving something in her hand, disrupting the line of customers. Overwhelmed with embarrassment, I looked at this crazy woman, my mother, who said, "You got accepted! You got accepted!"

When I got home from work, I read the letter from Edinboro University in detail. The letter from the Admissions Department offered me what Mr. King couldn't, options. I was accepted on a probationary basis and I would need to be in good academic standing at the end of my first semester to continue my dream.

After wading through grants, loans, and financial aid, I found myself a student at Edinboro University. Although I had achieved my dream of attending college, Mr. King's voice continued to take up space in my head. Even though Les Brown's teachings weren't part of my academic program, nor his concept of being hungry, I did have my grandmother Genevieve. On many levels, she channeled a lot of Les Brown's philosophies. My grandmother was so hungry to earn her degree that she traveled by train during the Great Depression. I, like her, made the conscious choice to do whatever was necessary to make the grades and graduate with a four-year degree from Edinboro University. I didn't understand it at the time, but I was HUNGRY for more. That hunger was the driving force. The voices and limiting beliefs were not going to win. I knew I needed to feed the voices of success if I was to earn my college degree.

While my college friends were partying, I was holed up in the library feeding my hunger, via

textbooks, highlighters, and massive amounts of coffee. That was my life in the first semester of my college years. It paid off when my college advisor told me at the end of that first semester, "Congratulations, you are a fully enrolled student. It was during winter break I shared the news with my grandmother. "I had no doubt," she exclaimed.

"One of the greatest investments you can make is in yourself."

After four years of continued investment in academics, I'm proud to say I graduated with a four-year degree, earning a bachelor's in social work. Like my grandmother, I had a passion for making a difference in the world. I continued to rewrite my story by completing my masters in counseling psychology, which rewarded me through the years with numerous career advancements. It was a long road from Mr.

King's office. Those years were a glorious time of discovering my self-worth and learning who I was as a person, or, as Les Brown refers to it, having "Greatness Within."

Helping Others Find Greatness

Once married, my husband and I embarked upon a move to expand our horizons. Suburban living in the beautiful state of Virginia was worlds apart from the small Pennsylvania town I had called home for three decades. I was working as a school counselor when our daughter was born in 2000. Like many, daycare became another parent and I longed to be home with my child. The day that changed everything, 9/11, only further solidified my desire to be the sole caretaker of my child. My maternal instincts kicked in like never before and I just wanted to spend time investing in our mother/child relationship.

It would take a few years after 9/11 and the birth of our son before the dream of being a stay-at-home mom would become a reality. The hunger I had felt in the early years of college and my career was reignited as a parent. When our son was nearly a year old and our daughter was almost three, my husband agreed and supported my longing to be home with our children. While my husband was the primary breadwinner for our family, I was the stay-at-home mom until they started school. I will be forever grateful for his support!

Whether it was volunteering at their school, extra-curricular activities, or arranging playdates, my highest hope for my children was that they would find their greatness within.

As the years passed, all our work paid off as our children gained their independence through their driver's licenses, graduating from high school, and applying for various colleges.

Dropping off my young adult children at their selected colleges was like looking in the mirror and feeling as if all the greatness had left me. Within a split second, I went from being out of the square to being trapped back in it again. Welcome to Empty Nesting, a club I didn't even know existed. All you have worked for and poured into is walking onto their college campus, moving into their first apartment, or flying across the country for their first job. The emptiness was overwhelming as well as overpowering. What happened to my greatness within? Did I mistakenly pack my greatness with my adult children's care package?

It was during this time that I learned that there was no manual on how to navigate the feelings of being an empty nester. After our children left our home, the expectation was to celebrate my new freedom and be productive and content. Instead, it was replaced with a feeling of profound loss, unexplained emptiness, and a lack of direction.

Through my journey of becoming an empty nester and re-discovering what greatness meant to me, I needed to ask myself several questions:

5. What voices am I listening to right now?
6. What voices do I need to let go of?
7. What voices do I need to hear now to rewrite the next chapter of my life?

Once I found the courage to answer the questions, I needed to come to fully understand, "Who am I without my children? Can I be happy with my newfound life? And what action steps do I need to achieve to answer the first two questions?

Once again, my life was filled with countless trials and tribulations. Once again, I chose to listen to the voice of my grandmother who had passed on but resides in the deepest recesses of my soul. I heard her say, "I have no doubt you will get through this too." As always, she was right.

My company, Empowering Life Coaching & Consulting, LLC. is my **Coming Full Square.** My Life Coaching program is the result of my journey through higher education, pushing through my own limiting beliefs and rewriting my story.

One of my greatest joys now is assisting others who are lost and need to be found.

"Wake up with passion and purpose and you'll never work a day in your life."

I am forever grateful to my long-time friends, my late grandmother, Genevieve, my mother, my father, my sister, my husband and now adult children for assisting me through the various stages of my life. Through their love, wisdom, and influence, I have become the person I am today.

You are never too old to set another goal or to dream a new dream.
                        -Les Brown, motivational speaker

Julie Duncan, Certified Master Life Coach, Transformation Academy
Empowering Life Coaching & Consulting, LLC
Website: julieduncancoaching.com
Email: julie@julieduncancoaching.com

About

ANDREA MASON

Andrea Mason is a woman of integrity and authenticity. She is your first choice, your global voice, certified global motivational speaker, and Alumna of Dr. Les Brown. She is your personal accountability coach and CEO of the life transformational journey, called, Press PLAY Plan Life According to You LLC. She has spoken globally on every continent amongst global elitists, leaders, kings, queens, and ambassadors on TV, radio, and podcasts. She featured speaker at Latino World Travel Fest and in several global magazines, and Amazon's #1 best-selling author to an international anthology. She coaches children, men, women, and families worldwide, and goes back to her roots speaking in orphanages, as a former adoptee.

She is a global ambassador, helping people learn how to become their authentic selves and lead an authentic life. She is a host of the podcast, Unleashing the Champion Within, and recently released her book, Victim to Victorious.

Chapter 9
"A journey of resilience and transformation"

 Andrea Mason

 am.andreamasons

 www.andreamasons.com

128

A Journey of Resilience and Transformation

Andrea Mason

Early Life Challenges

I came into this world fighting. Born during the height of the Colombian cartel, my birth parents made the ultimate sacrifice. They put me up for adoption, hoping to give me a shot at a better life. At just 11 months old and weighing only 11 pounds, I was taken in by my American parents. They wrapped me in their loving arms and never let go.

Growing up, I quickly learned that being different came with a price. Kids can be cruel, and boy, were they cruel to me. "You're adopted," they'd taunt. "If your real parents didn't love you, who will?" Their words stung like a thousand needles, leaving scars I'd carry for years.

To cope, I threw myself into sports and music. On the soccer field, I could outrun my pain. At the piano, I could drown out the noise. But no matter how much I excelled, I always felt like an outsider looking in.

Despite the darkness, a small flame began to flicker inside me. I wanted to make a difference in the world of mental health. I saw firsthand how much suffering emotional trauma could cause, and I vowed to be a voice for the voiceless. I didn't know it then, but that sense of purpose would be my lifeline in the years to come.

As I navigated my own healing journey, I quickly learned that even the strongest among us can crumble under the weight of heartbreak. And my greatest test was just around the corner.

Pivotal Moments of Change

Life has a funny way of throwing curveballs when you least expect them. For me, that curveball came in the form of losing my mom in 2007. She was my rock, my confidante, my everything. When she passed away, it felt like the ground beneath my feet had crumbled, leaving me in a free fall with no end in sight.

I tried to push through the pain, to keep going like nothing had changed. But by 2016, I hit rock bottom. I was a shell of my former self, going through the motions but feeling nothing. It was like I was watching my life from the outside, powerless to change the trajectory I was on.

And then, the wake-up call came. I landed in the hospital, my body ravaged by years of neglect and emotional turmoil. As I lay there, hooked up to machines and facing my own mortality, something shifted inside me. I realized that I had a choice. I could either let my pain consume me, or I could use it as fuel to transform my life.

I chose the latter. With every fiber of my being, I made the decision to rewrite my story. No longer would I be a victim of my circumstances. No longer would I let my past define me. I was going to take back control, one day at a time.

It wasn't easy. I had to confront the limiting beliefs and self-sabotaging behaviors that had held me back for so long. I had to learn to trust again, to open myself up to the possibility of healing and growth. There were days when I wanted to give up, to retreat back into the familiar comfort of my pain. But I knew that I couldn't go back. I had come too far to turn back now.

Through self-realization, self-awareness, self-discovery, mindfulness, and a whole lot of self-reflection, I began to peel back the layers of my trauma. I learned to reframe my failures as opportunities for growth, to see my scars as badges of honor rather than sources of shame. Slowly but surely, I began to reclaim my power, my voice, and my sense of self.

Looking back, I can see that those pivotal moments of change were the catalysts I needed to transform my life. They forced me to confront my deepest fears, to question everything I thought I knew, and to rebuild myself from the ground up. And though the journey was far from easy, I wouldn't trade it for the world. Because it led me to the most important discovery of all: the strength and resilience that had been inside me all along.

Discovering My Purpose

As I began to heal and grow, I felt a new sense of purpose stirring within me. I knew that my experiences, painful as they were, had given me a unique perspective on life. I had been through the fire and come out the other side, and I wanted to use that hard-won wisdom to help others.

I started by sharing my story, first with a few close friends and then with larger audiences. Every time I spoke, I could see the impact my words had on people. They would come up to me afterwards, tears in their eyes, and thank me for giving voice to their own struggles. It was like a light bulb went off in my head. This was what I was meant to do.

With a renewed sense of determination, I threw myself into my new mission. I honed my skills as a listener and communicator, learning how to create safe spaces for others to share their own stories. I studied psychology and human behavior, seeking to understand the complex ways in which we are all interconnected.

As I began to work with people from all walks of life, I was struck by the common threads that ran through all of our experiences. No matter where we came from or what we had been through, we all shared the same basic desires: to be seen, heard, and valued for who we are.

I made it my mission to help people tap into their

own inner strength and resilience. I wanted to show them that they had the power to transform their lives, just as I had transformed mine. And so, I began to share the tools and strategies that had worked for me – things like mindfulness, self-care, and positive self-talk.

As I continued on this path, I began to see the ripple effects of my work. People who had once felt hopeless and alone were now finding their own sense of purpose and direction. They were breaking free from the chains of their past and stepping into their own power. And with each success story, my own sense of fulfillment grew.

But I knew that I couldn't stop there. I wanted to take my message to a broader audience, to reach as many people as possible. And so, I made the decision to become a global speaker and coach. It was a huge leap of faith, but I knew in my heart that it was the right path for me.

As I embarked on this new chapter of my journey, I was filled with a sense of excitement and possibility. I knew that there would be challenges and obstacles along the way, but I also knew that I had the strength and resilience to overcome them. And with each new connection I made, each new story I heard, I felt more and more certain that I was exactly where I was meant to be.

Looking back now, I can see that discovering my purpose was not a single moment, but a series of small steps that led me to where I am today. It was a journey of self-discovery, of learning to trust my own instincts and intuition. And though the road was not always easy, I am grateful for every twist and turn. Because it led me to a life that is more fulfilling and meaningful than I ever could have imagined.

Lessons Learned and Insights Gained

Now, I know what you might be thinking. "Andrea, all this talk about purpose and transformation sounds great, but how do I actually make it happen in my own life?" Well, let me tell you, it's not about some grand gesture or overnight success. It's about the small, daily choices we make to show up for ourselves and others.

One of the biggest lessons I've learned on this journey is the power of mindset. Our thoughts and beliefs shape our reality in ways we often don't even realize. For so long, I was trapped in a cycle of negative self-talk and limiting beliefs. I told myself I wasn't good enough, that I didn't deserve happiness or success. But as I began to challenge those beliefs and replace them with more empowering ones, my whole world began to shift.

Another key insight I've gained is the importance of authenticity and integrity. In a world that often feels like it's all about keeping up appearances, it can be scary to show up as our true selves. But when we do, when we let our guard down and allow ourselves to be seen, magic happens. We connect with others on a deeper level, we build trust and rapport, and we create space for real transformation to occur.

Of course, none of this is easy. It takes courage to be vulnerable, to own our stories and our struggles. But I've learned that vulnerability is not a weakness, it's a strength. When we have the courage to share our truth, we give others permission to do the same. We create a ripple effect of healing and growth that extends far beyond ourselves.

As I've continued on this path, I've also come to realize the importance of surrounding myself with people who lift me up and support my growth. We are the sum of the five people we spend the most time with, and I've made a conscious effort to seek out individuals who inspire me, challenge me, and hold me accountable to my highest self.

But perhaps the most important lesson I've learned is that we are all a work in progress. There is no finish line, no moment of arrival when we can say "I've made it." Growth and transformation are a lifelong journey, and the key is to embrace the process, to find joy in the little moments along the way. "Dreams don't have deadlines, they create destinations" ` Andrea Mason

So, if you're reading this and feeling stuck, know that you are not alone. Know that you have the power to change your story, to create a life that feels authentic and fulfilling. It won't happen overnight, and it won't always be easy. But I promise you this: it will be worth it.

Because when you start living life on your own terms, when you show up as your true self and let your light shine, amazing things start to happen. You attract people and opportunities that align with your values and your purpose. You find a sense of meaning and fulfillment that goes beyond anything external. You become the hero of your own story.

And that, my friend, is what this journey is all about. It's about claiming your power, owning your truth, and creating a life that sets your soul on fire. So keep going, keep growing, and know that you've got this. Because the world needs your light, now more than ever.

Living My Best Life

If you had told me 10 years ago that I'd be where I am today, I would've laughed in your face. Back then, I was a mess. I was stuck in a cycle of self-destruction, numbing my pain with anything I could find. I had no idea who I was or what I wanted out of life. But here's the thing: hitting rock bottom was the best thing that ever happened to me.

It forced me to take a long, hard look at myself and my choices. It made me realize that if I wanted something different, I had to be willing to do the work. And so, I did. I got honest with myself, I sought out help, and I started putting one foot in front of the other.

Fast forward to today, and I am living a life beyond

my wildest dreams. I wake up every morning excited to face the day, knowing that I get to do work that lights me up and makes a real difference in people's lives. I have a tribe of amazing friends and supporters who lift me up and challenge me to be my best self. And most importantly, I have a relationship with myself that is built on love, respect, and unwavering self-compassion.

Now, let me be clear: this doesn't mean that every day is sunshine and rainbows. I still have my struggles and my setbacks, just like everyone else. But the difference is that I now have the tools and the mindset to navigate those challenges with grace and resilience.

I've learned to embrace the journey, to find joy and purpose in the present moment, even when things aren't perfect. I've learned to let go of the need to control everything and trust that the universe has my back. And I've learned that true happiness comes not from external validation or material success, but from a deep sense of inner peace and alignment.

So, what does living my best life look like on a practical level? It means taking care of myself first and foremost - physically, mentally, emotionally, and spiritually. It means surrounding myself with people who inspire me and support my growth. It means setting boundaries and saying no to things that don't serve me. And it means showing up every day as the best version of myself, even when it's hard.

But perhaps most importantly, living my best life means using my story and my experiences to make a positive impact on the world. It means being a voice for the voiceless, a beacon of faith for those who are still struggling. It means shining my light as brightly as I can and inspiring others to do the same.

Because at the end of the day, that's what this journey is all about. It's about connection, it's about growth, and it's about leaving the world a little bit better than we found it. And I truly believe that when we commit to living our best lives, anything becomes possible.

So, if you're reading this and feeling like your best life is still out of reach, know that you are not alone. Know that you have the power to change your story, one choice at a time. And know that every step you take, every obstacle you overcome, is bringing you closer to the life you deserve.

Keep going, keep growing, and trust the journey. Because your best life is waiting for you. And I promise you, it's even better than you can imagine.

Embracing the Journey

You know, one of the biggest misconceptions about personal growth is that there's some kind of endpoint, a moment when we can say "I've arrived" and coast from there on out. But the truth is, growth is a lifelong journey. There's no finish line, no moment of ultimate enlightenment where we have it all figured out.

And you know what? That's a good thing. Because it means that every day, we have the opportunity to learn, to expand, to become more fully ourselves. It means that no matter where we are on our path, there's always room for more growth, more discovery, more joy.

For me, embracing this journey has been a game changer. It's allowed me to let go of the pressure to have it all figured out and instead, focus on showing up as my best self in each moment. It's given me permission to be imperfect, to make mistakes, and to trust that every experience is a chance to learn and grow.

One of the biggest lessons I've learned on this journey is the power of gratitude. When we focus on what we're grateful for, when we take the time to appreciate the blessings in our lives, everything shifts. We start to see challenges as opportunities, obstacles as chances to grow. We find joy in the little moments and peace in the present.

Another key insight I've gained is the importance of self-love and self-care. For so long, I put everyone else's needs before my own, thinking that was the way to be a good person. But now I know that taking care of myself is not selfish, it's essential. When I fill my own cup first, I have so much more to give to others.

Of course, embracing the journey doesn't mean that every day is easy. There are still times when I struggle, when I doubt myself or feel overwhelmed by the challenges I face. But what's different now is that

I have a toolbox of strategies and mindsets to help me navigate those tough times.

I've learned to lean into my support system, to reach out for help when I need it and to surround myself with people who lift me up. I've learned to reframe my thoughts, to focus on what I can control, and to let go of what I can't. And I've learned to trust the process, to have faith that even the darkest moments are leading me somewhere meaningful.

Because that's the thing about growth: it's not always comfortable. It can be messy and scary and downright painful at times. But on the other side of that discomfort is a life beyond your wildest dreams. A life filled with purpose, passion, and unshakeable inner peace.

So if you're in the thick of it right now, if you're facing challenges that feel insurmountable, know that you're not alone. Know that every hero's journey includes moments of doubt and despair. But also know that you have the strength, the courage, and the resilience to keep going.

Embrace the journey, trust the process, and never forget how far you've come. Because your story is far from over. And the best is yet to come.

Embracing Your Power and Shining Your Light

If there's one thing I've learned on this journey, it's that we all have a story to tell. We all have unique experiences, struggles, and triumphs that have shaped us into who we are today. And when we have the courage to share those stories, to be vulnerable and authentic, we open the door for incredible growth and connection.

So, my friend, that's my invitation to you today. To embrace your own story, to own your truth, and to start living a life that sets your soul on fire. Because the world needs your light, your gifts, your unique perspective. And you deserve to live a life that feels authentic and fulfilling.

Now, I know that can feel scary. Trust me, I've been there. It's easy to get caught up in fear, in self-doubt, in the voices that tell us we're not good enough or that we have to fit into some predetermined box. But here's the thing: those voices are liars. And the only way to silence them is to take action, to start showing up as your true self, one small step at a time.

So start by getting clear on what you want. What does your best life look like? What makes you come alive? What kind of impact do you want to have on the world? Write it down, create a vision board, do whatever it takes to get crystal clear on your dreams and desires.

Then, start taking action. Start saying yes to the things that light you up and no to the things that drain you. Start surrounding yourself with people who support and inspire you. Start making self-care a non-negotiable priority. And start sharing your story, even if it's just with one trusted friend or in the pages of your journal.

Because here's the thing: every single one of us has the power to create change, to make a difference, to leave a legacy. But it starts with believing in ourselves, in our own unique journey and purpose. It starts with having the courage to take that first step, even when we're scared.

And I promise you, it's so worth it. Because when you start living life on your own terms, when you align with your true self and your deepest passions, magic happens. You start attracting the right people, the right opportunities, the right resources to support you on your path. And you start feeling a sense of joy, fulfillment, and inner peace that nothing external can shake.

So my friend, this is my call to action for you today. To step into your power, to embrace your story, and to start creating the life you truly desire. It won't be easy, and it won't happen overnight. But I promise you, it will be the most rewarding journey you ever take.

And know that you're not alone. Know that there's a whole community of people out there cheering you on, ready to support you and celebrate your progress. Including me. Because I believe in you, and I know that you have everything you need to create a life beyond your wildest dreams.

So take that first step. Trust the journey. And never, ever give up on yourself. Because your best life is waiting for you. And it's time to claim it.

Remember, "through life's adversities, you have the choice to create your own identity". In the realm of personal growth and accountability, few voices resonate as profoundly as the one I use.

My life's work, encapsulated in the innovative Press PLAY Plan Life According to You LLC, stands as a testament to the power of transformation through forgiveness and accountability. My journey is one of remarkable resilience and unwavering commitment to helping others achieve personal freedom. My quote, "Anything You've Gone Through, Gives You the Certification to Help Someone Else Overcome It, Too!" is not just a statement; it's a philosophy that underpins my entire coaching ethos. Follow Your Heart Not the Herd Nor the Hurt, for Success and Joyfulness are on the other side." ~ Andrea Mason

ABOUT

BRIANNA THAXTON

Brianna grew up the youngest of seven children with their single mother. They had very little finances until their mom completed schooling and got a job as a nurse. Influenced by both mother and grandmother who worked hard, she always pressed through to find a way.

Finding herself in a toxic marriage that was leaving her feeling without value or purpose, she had to learn to overcome and change the direction of her life when she was at rock bottom. She then studied extensively to better herself and took action to overcome life's challenges.

With her faith In God as her rock foundation she found a sense of greater purpose for life. She is now dedicated to discovering what that is, and always walking towards it, while also encouraging others to seek out and fulfill their own life purpose.

Chapter 10
"Overcoming challenges
with faith & action"

 Brianna Thaxton

 briannathaxtoncoaching

 www.briannathaxton.com

Overcoming Challenges with Faith & Action

Brianna Thaxton

What challenge is blocking you from moving forward into your purpose? We all face challenges in life. To put them into perspective, I like to look at them as mountains to be overcome.

How we overcome every struggle is based on our mindset and faith. These two things truly go hand-in-hand. We can wish it gone, complain about it, and even pray about it. However, without faith and action that mountain will stay. And it will block you from becoming all that you were meant to be.

Challenges always seem to come suddenly and unexpectedly. Sure, you may know your life isn't perfect, but it was flowing and you didn't think it was too far beyond average. You have your home, your family, the people you love and who love you. Everything seems okay by life's general standards. There may be rough days, but you always get through them.

Then one day, without warning, the curtain gets ripped down and your life is exposed to you in ways you didn't even envision. What you believed about your life wasn't reality.

Hit by the Bus of Life

Sometimes our challenges are mountains we need to climb, but other times they can feel like getting hit by a bus. I remember the day I was hit by my bus. It crashed into me and left me feeling beyond hope.

At the time, My then-husband was working out of the state for weeks at a time in the oil fields. I was a stay-at-home mama with three incredible babies keeping me busy full-time. When my husband was gone, I felt so alone managing our home by myself. So,we purchased a small travel trailer where we could go with him. Our first trip: Wyoming.

On our way to Wyoming, life felt as it should be. Our family was cruising down the road on a beautiful sunny day. Endless fields stretched out as far as the eye could see. Our family was going to be staying together as he worked out-of-state. It was perfect.

But things took a sudden turn. A side window on our travel trailer flew open and shattered. I grabbed my phone to look up glass repair along our route, but quickly realized my internet wouldn't connect. I asked my husband if his phone's internet was working, and surprisingly it was. He let me use his phone to search for glass repair places. But, as I began to type in the search browser, a history of past searches appeared.

Instantly I could feel my throat knotting up, my body went numb, my brain couldn't even process what I was seeing.

I was not his only woman.

I knew our marriage wasn't perfect, but I always thought he was such a respectable guy. I never expected this. Needing to know what was going on behind the scenes in my marriage, I asked about what I was seeing and was met with lies.

Have you ever given your everything for someone, just to be taken advantage of, used, and walked over? When it's someone you love, it can leave you in a dark place. You are left trying to figure out how to pick up the pieces and put your life back together again.

As a Christian, I felt it was my duty to forgive. And to be honest, I was afraid to get a divorce. I was afraid of what others would think and I wanted to stay for our kids.

But I was operating from fear. And it left me spinning. I couldn't figure out if I should get a divorce or hold out for the possibility that it would get better. In the meantime, life was passing me by.

Standing at Life's Crossroads

The way we respond to life's challenges comes from our mindset. When you're at a crossroads in life and you're not sure which way to go, it can become paralyzing. So many of us get stuck because we never learned how to move forward. I've learned if you can't figure out how to move forward, it's possible something in your past is holding you back.

We all develop our own patterns of facing life's problems throughout our childhood. Trace the line back through your life to see why you are facing your challenges the way you are.

Trace It Back...

Although I was facing what many say would be an end-all for them, I felt stuck. I had believed I would never put up with cheating, and yet here I was, staying in my marriage after my husband's betrayal. I couldn't understand at the time, but there were things from my past that were keeping me in an unhealthy marriage.

You see, my mother left my dad when I was a baby, after enduring years of mental, emotional, and physical abuse. She's an incredible woman, who raised seven kids as a single mother, and never gave up. I have a great relationship with my mother, who has inspired me to keep going in life. But I never had any meaningful relationship with my dad.

As a young girl, our brief supervised visits always felt like I was going to visit a stranger. When I was old enough, I knew I didn't want a relationship with him based on his character. Even at a young age, I knew it was better for me not to have my dad directly as a part of my life. However, it left me feeling like I was missing something in my life.

Can you relate? I know many people, who struggle with feelings of low self-worth, can trace it back, at least in part, to something from their childhood. It could be an absent parent, an abusive parent, or bullying in school. Whatever the challenge, we develop a lot of our ideas about ourselves based on how people treat us as children. It took until adulthood to understand, but for me a lot of it stemmed from not having a healthy father figure in my life.

Unfortunately, there are nearly 20-million children growing up in single-parent homes. The family unit was designed to provide a full system of love and support around us. When we don't have this, we begin to feel like we are somehow inadequate. Like there is something lacking in us. As children facing this feeling of lack, we often relate it back as something wrong with ourselves.

For me, I started comparing myself to other girls. They seemed prettier, more popular, cooler, and funnier. Whereas I was tall and skinny as a stick. Couple this with comments I received from others about my looks and I became extremely self-conscious.

I remember one day my grandpa was visiting. The family was all outside eating and here is dear sweet grandpa. He reminded me of a huge Hulk-Hogan type with his cut-off jean shorts and sleeveless shirt. He even had the white handlebar mustache with matching white hair pulled back into a ponytail.

But he said something to me that I have never forgotten. He said, "If you turn sideways and stick out your tongue, you'd look like a zipper." I'll be honest, it took me a while to grasp the meaning, but he was calling me skinny in a whole new way that hurt me to the core.

Looking back, some people may think it was funny and not a big deal. But at this young age I had already heard so many comments about my body that it just added more insult to injury.

You Deserve Better

Just as some girls do when they reach a certain age, almost overnight I went from being insecure about my looks to getting a lot of attention from boys. Granted, this was not the kind of attention I really wanted. There is a big difference between a sleazy "compliment" with underlying motives and a respectful compliment.

So many young girls put up with this because they are not taught their own worth. When someone pays any kind of attention to them it causes them to feel "desired" by others. They equate this type of attention with their value. You don't feel like or even realize you deserve better.

In fact, you think you should be happy that someone even wants to be around you (even if they don't treat you well). You rationalize with yourself about how you're being treated and it leaves you without any boundaries to protect your self-esteem. My poor boundaries and self-respect carried over into my marriage, causing unspeakable heartache.

But I believe there has to be a point where we look at our lives and say...

"This isn't what I want. I want more than this and I deserve better."

Discovering Faith

Although raised in church, I always believed God was out there somewhere beyond the stars. I definitely didn't think He was here with us until one life-altering day in elementary school.

I think I was in 5th grade, but one day I popped a Red-Hot Fireball candy into my mouth as I stepped off the school bus. Now, we were not allowed to have candy on the bus, but I was feeling a little rebellious. So I snuck that candy into my mouth and a split-second later, that candy lodged in my throat.

I couldn't cough. I couldn't breathe. I couldn't speak.

Frantic, I turned around to the bus, which was still sitting parked about 30 feet away. I was about to take a step towards it when I saw the doors close as it pulled away.

I turned towards my friends and watched as they rounded the corner and disappeared. I was completely alone.

I started down the road towards my home. Something told me not to run. Somehow at my young age I felt that if I ran, it would use up the oxygen I still had faster, and I wouldn't make it.

So, I took slow, thoughtful steps as I walked and looked around at the trailer houses that filled this street. I was desperately trying to find any house that showed signs of someone being home.

But, everywhere I turned was silent and still. The edge of my vision was slowly being overtaken on all sides by a dark cloud. I tried the Heimlich maneuver on myself. With my right hand I pressed my left fist up and under my ribs repeatedly, trying to dislodge the candy, but it had no effect.

The darkness was edging in more and more. I still couldn't breathe. I was losing hope, until I had this thought: Pray.

I closed my eyes and asked Jesus to "please save me". And with unbelievable speed, that Red-Hot Fireball launched out of my throat and hit the pavement so hard it shattered into pieces. I was in shock.

This was something I will never forget. And it showed me that God does see us, and He hears our prayers. Since that time, I have had so many incredible experiences in my life that I know God is with each and every one of us. In the most challenging times of our lives, when we feel we won't make it through, sometimes all it takes is calling out to God.

Knowing that God promises to never leave you doesn't necessarily make everything easier. Just don't forget that He's there for you, and you can make it through. Even if you don't feel Him, I can promise He is right there waiting for you to call out. If you can learn to trust this, you will be able to overcome anything that life throws at you. You will make it.

"If you want people to respect you, you have to first respect yourself."

As a wife and mother, I had tied my self-worth and value to my children and marriage. I gave all of myself to my marriage, even to the point of allowing myself to be disrespected. I felt like the goal was to keep my marriage together at all costs.

When I realized I had been cheated on, lied to, and manipulated, that superficial feeling of self-worth and value came crashing down. I had tied my self-worth to my status as the wife of this man that I thought was absolutely amazing. However, I had been giving so much of myself and not respecting myself enough to expect the same level of love and respect in return. How could I honestly expect someone to give me more respect than I was giving myself? If you want people to respect you, you have to first respect yourself. So, I had to reflect deeply:

"If I am at this point in my life right now, what will it be like in 5 or 10 years?"

It's so important to reflect on your life and ask yourself the same thing. Do you want to continue on the same path you've been on, or do you want to change the course? You have the power to do that!

Sometimes choosing to change the direction of your life, or to face your battles, can be daunting when you feel like you have to face them alone. For me it became easier when I learned to trust God through the process of learning to respect myself.

Learn to Take Responsibility

How did I end up here? I had to take a hard look at my life and realize that I was in this mess, not just because of my husband's behavior. If I'm honest with myself, I played a huge role in it all.

I didn't understand my insecurities. I didn't address my low sense of self-worth. I didn't know how to have a true, deep relationship. I thought if I fell in love and married a guy that had similar interests and said he had the same morals and values, then everything would be amazing.

But, when things went sour, I didn't know how to handle it. I lowered my expectations in my marriage to match the treatment I was getting, when I should have been setting healthy boundaries and having respect for myself. I had gone off track from the way I knew I wanted to live my life in order to please other people and feel some sense of value.

Have you ever done that in a relationship? Where you've gotten off track at some point in order to not derail the train of your relationship. You're not alone there!

It's important not to beat yourself up when you're there. Just figure out where you went off track and what needs to change. God has enough grace for you, so don't give up on yourself when you slip, or you'll never get where you're meant to be.

I realized I had quickly married a man I barely knew. I assumed things about him because my emotions were flying high. I overlooked red flags and hung on his every word, even if they didn't match his actions. And when my emotions mixed with my insecurities, it was easy for me to jump into a situation that wasn't for my highest good. But now that I knew my self-worth, I could learn how to respect myself so it wouldn't wreak havoc with my relationships anymore.

You're Not Stuck Here...

Life is full of struggles, challenges, and heartbreaks. Don't get stuck in them. After discovering my husband's betrayal, there were times I didn't think I could keep going. I felt stuck trying to keep my marriage together. I found myself hoping and believing that every "sorry" would be the turning point in our marriage.

It was a constant pattern of highs and lows. So many people stay- holding out for the next "good" time. But, I finally saw that my life couldn't move forward as long as I stayed on this mental and emotional roller coaster.

I had to release the past and stop reliving the painful experiences in my head. I had to shift my focus from what was wrong in my marriage and my life. Because the more we focus on what's wrong, the more it wears us down. It slowly erodes our peace and steals our joy. You lose hope for a better future and become a miserable shell of who you once were.

I had stayed for 8 more years, going through 2 counselors, watching endless videos, and reading tons of books and articles about relationships, marriage, infidelity trying to save my marriage. So, the hardest thing was realizing that I really couldn't do it all on my own.

Because of my faith, I was paralyzed with fear of getting a divorce. I worried that God would hate me. I worried about my kids' futures because I knew firsthand the negative effects of not having a father in my life.

But when I asked myself how things would be if I stayed, I knew the answer was clear. God had a plan, purpose and path for my life, and I wasn't walking it.

So, after years of praying, working on myself and in my relationship with God, I finally moved past my fears and doubts. I knew the only way to find out what my purpose was, was to go after it.

So finally, I left that toxic marriage. And using the lessons I learned from the experience, I started my own coaching business helping others overcome their challenges, develop the understanding and worth of their own value, and finally walk a life of purpose and meaning.

When I'm coaching people who are feeling stuck by a challenge, I encourage them to ask:

- "Why am I holding on to this?"
- "Is it helpful for me to dwell on this?"
- "How can I change this?"
- "What do I want my future to be like?"
- "What is the very first step I need to take to move in that direction?"
- "Is this helping my relationship with God or separating me from Him?"

It's crucial to put things into perspective: focus on the long term. Even more so, focus on the eternal things rather than temporary. Everything that we experience in this life is temporary.

For me it all boils down to this: Jesus said the most important commandment is to love God with all your heart and the second is to love your neighbor as yourself. This means: Love God, Love Yourself, and Love Others. Because you can't love others equally, if you don't first love yourself. Keeping this perspective helps us to make better decisions in the here and now.

What I Want for You

We don't always know what our next move should be.

This is where faith comes in. God has created you for a very specific purpose. As long as you're staying trapped by the challenge you're facing, you will never walk in your purpose.

For me, I had to face the ugly reality that divorce was what I needed to endure, in order to move forward. I knew God had a calling on my life and I couldn't see how to walk in it while I was in that marriage.

"Having a knowledge of your purpose and not walking in it, is worse than not knowing you have a purpose."

When you don't know that you have a purpose, you are blissfully unaware of something greater that you could be walking in. When you do know that you have a purpose, then you have to face yourself. You have to ask: "Why am I not walking in the incredible thing I was created for?"

Are you going to ignore your calling or go all in to live out a life of purpose and meaning?

I had to come to a point where I knew that I had tried everything that I could to save my marriage, and it wasn't working. I had to admit to myself that I was created for more. I had to get over my own insecurities that were causing me to stay.

I could keep facing that mountain and believe there's nothing beyond it, with no hope for a better future... OR I could face that mountain with faith and tell it to move.

Jesus said, in Matthew 17:20, that if you have faith the size of a mustard seed, you can tell that mountain to move. You can overcome anything through faith. You just have to want it and believe that nothing is impossible for you. Then follow through with action.

I faced my mountain. Even though I couldn't see past it, I chose to believe something better was out there for me - on the other side of that mountain. It was terrifying, but it set me free. I had to step forward in faith and believe God would take care of me and my children and He has in incredible ways!

You'd be surprised what God will do to help you when you choose to move forward with blind faith and trust Him.

I went from being an insecure empty shell of who I once was, to having an abundance of amazing friends and support. I've been blessed to help start and lead ministries. I've started a coaching and speaking business to empower others to overcome their challenges through faith and a mindset shift. I've traveled across the country going to business and speaking conferences.

I promise, no matter how difficult your challenges are right now, you don't have to stay there, in the place where they have you trapped. You only need a new perspective. You need to figure out what is keeping you stuck.

For me, it was a low sense of self-worth and a lack of faith. I had to accept that I am fearfully and wonderfully made, and so are you. I had to believe that God had a plan and purpose for my life that was far bigger than I could ever imagine. I am now a speaker, coach and author.

He has that for you too! Your value is far greater than you know. You are an incredible person and you have an amazing future, you just can't see it from the other side of the mountain. Don't let your past, your failures, your insecurities or the way others treat you keep you from walking in your amazing life.

Your future is right here and right now, it just takes that first step.

ABOUT

TONEY JENKINS

According to author Toney Jenkins, "Everyone is a winner, in my book!"

Faith in God is what governs how he operates, his outlook and his expectation to receive everything God says he can have. Toney lives without fear and moves with the speed of instruction to maximize his life and the lives of those closely associated with him.

A former Regional Vice President in corporate America, professional athlete and entrepreneur for over 25 years, Toney has made his mark on the lives of thousands of families he has helped obtain their path to financial freedom and on the businesses served by his company, Fit Technology and Transport LLC.

Chapter 11
"Failing forward: turning failure into fit success"

⬤ Toney Jenkins
in i_made_it_then_i_didnt

FAILING FORWARD: TURNING FAILURE INTO FIT SUCCESS

TONEY JENKINS

Did you know that self-doubt often starts as a tiny seed, planted in the fertile soil of our minds? It's a pesky little thing, easily overlooked at first. But if left unchecked, it can grow into a tangled web of limiting beliefs that hold us back from reaching our full potential or our fit success.

For me, those seeds were planted early on. Growing up as a young African American boy, I found myself constantly fighting against stereotypes and societal expectations. The world seemed to have a predetermined notion of who I was supposed to be and what I was capable of achieving.

Can you remember a time when you felt like the odds were stacked against you? When it seemed like everyone around you had already decided what your future would look like? It was a suffocating feeling.

I knew deep down that I wanted to be great, to be elite, to be the best at whatever I put my mind to. But there was always this nagging voice in the back of my head, whispering, "Toney, can you really be the best? Are you putting in enough work to truly excel?"

Those doubts had a way of creeping in, like uninvited guests at a dinner party. They'd make themselves comfortable, settling into the corners of my mind, and before I knew it, they were dictating my every move. This is why positive self-talk is crucial to achieving your fit success.

The Comparison Trap

You might remember a time when you found yourself constantly comparing your journey to those around you. It's a dangerous game, isn't it? Measuring your worth based on the accomplishments of others. It's an easy trap to distract you from seeing your small wins and improvements.

For me, it was working alongside brilliantly talented individuals at Fortune 500 companies. I'd sit in rooms filled with intelligent, successful people and feel that pang of self-doubt creeping in. I couldn't help but wonder if I truly belonged there, if my intellect and abilities were on par with my colleagues.

It's easy to fall into the comparison trap, to benchmark yourself against others and feel like you're coming up short. But here's the thing: comparison is a thief of joy. It robs you of the ability to appreciate your own unique talents and strengths.

I had to learn to silence that inner critic, and to stop measuring my worth based on the accomplishments of others. I realized that my journey and measure of success was my own, and as long as I was putting in the work and striving to be the best version of myself, that was enough.

Rising Above Expectations

Think about a time when someone doubted your abilities when they placed limitations on what they believed you could achieve. That could be a heavy weight to carry. The burden of others' expectations limits your creativity and your ability to be you.

As an African American man living in America I've faced my fair share of doubters. There were those who believed that my success would be limited and that I couldn't compete at the highest levels. As a young boy, they would see my skin color and make assumptions about my academic capabilities.

But I refused to let their doubts define me. I knew that I had a choice: I could either accept their limited vision of my future, or I could rise above it and prove them wrong.

So I put in the work. I pushed myself harder. I studied, I learned, I grew. And slowly but surely, I started shattering those stereotypes. I excelled in school, sports and in my business career. I am now taking on leadership roles and making a name for myself in the financial industry.

It wasn't easy, and there were moments when the doubts would try to creep back in. But I learned to use those faith and positive self-talk as fuel, as motivation to keep pushing forward. I realized that every time I proved a doubter wrong, I was not only validating my own abilities but also paving the way for others who looked like me.

The Power of Positive Self-Talk

Have you ever noticed how the words you say to yourself can have a profound impact on your beliefs and actions? The way we talk to ourselves matters more than we often realize.

For years, I allowed negative self-talk to run rampant in my mind. I'd tell myself things like, "You're not smart enough," or "You don't have what it takes to succeed." Those words became a self-fulfilling prophecy, holding me back from reaching my full potential.

But then I learned the power of positive self-talk. I started consciously rewriting the script in my mind, replacing those negative thoughts with empowering affirmations. Instead of telling myself I couldn't do something, I'd say, "You've got this, Toney. You have the skills and the determination to make it happen."

It's amazing how a simple shift in our internal dialogue can change everything. When you become your own biggest cheerleader, when you start believing in yourself and speaking life into your dreams, there's no limit to what you can achieve.

I remember a specific moment when the power of positive self-talk really hit home for me. I was preparing for a big presentation at work, and the doubts were creeping in. I started to question whether I was truly prepared, whether I had what it took to impress my colleagues and superiors.

But then I caught myself and decided to change the

narrative. I stood in front of the mirror, looked myself in the eye, and said, "Toney, you've put in the work. You know your stuff. You're going to walk into that room and knock it out of the park."

And you know what? I did. The presentation went better than I could have imagined, and I walked out of that room feeling like I could conquer the world. That's the power of positive self-talk. It's like having a personal hype squad in your own mind, cheering you on and reminding you of your greatness.

The Influence of Your Inner Circle

Did you know that the people you surround yourself with can have a significant impact on your self-belief and success? The energy and attitudes of those closest to us have a way of rubbing off, for better or for worse.

I realized early on that if I wanted to achieve greatness, I needed to surround myself with individuals who were striving for the same thing. I prayed for mentors and advocates, people who believed in me and would be willing to invest their time with me to allow me to become my best self.

By surrounding myself with positive influences, with people who had already achieved the kind of success I aspired to, I started to see myself in a new light. Their belief in me became a mirror, reflecting back the potential and greatness that had been inside me all along.

It's easy to underestimate the power of our inner circle, to brush off the impact that others can have on our mindset and beliefs. But I've learned that the people we choose to surround ourselves with, like-minded dreamers, can easily start lifting themselves up.

So take a moment to reflect on your own inner circle. Are the people in your life supporting your dreams and encouraging you to be your best self? Or are they filling your mind with doubts and limiting beliefs? This is an important piece to your fit success puzzle, do not rust this part.

If you find that your inner circle is holding you back, don't be afraid to make some changes. Seek out individuals who inspire you, who challenge you to grow and push past your comfort zone. Surround yourself with positivity, and watch as your self-belief and confidence soar to new heights.

Remember, you are the sum of the five people you spend the most time with. Choose those people wisely, and let their belief in you become a catalyst for your own greatness.

Stepping Outside Your Comfort Zone

Can you remember a time when you were faced with a decision that terrified you? A moment when you had to choose between staying in your comfort zone or taking a leap of faith into the unknown?

For me, that moment came when I was fired from my corporate job which forced me into my passion of entrepreneurship. It was risky, a step into uncharted territory, and I had no time for self doubt.

I knew that growth and comfort rarely coexist. If I wanted to achieve the level of success I dreamed of, I had to be forced out of my comfort zone. God knew that the only way to get me to leave my comfortable Regional Vice President title was to force me out. So, in a matter of hours, I went from an employee to the boss. I stepped outside my comfort zone and started my own business. It was scary, but with each challenge I faced, with each obstacle I overcame, I could feel myself growing stronger and more confident.

Embracing change, stepping outside your comfort zone, is never easy. But it's in those moments of discomfort that we truly discover what we're capable of. It's where we shed the layers of self-doubt and emerge as the best versions of ourselves.

Think about a time when you took a chance on yourself, when you dared to venture into the unknown. Maybe it was applying for a job you felt underqualified for, or speaking up in a meeting when you would usually stay silent. Whatever it was, I bet you felt a mix of fear and exhilaration, a rush of adrenaline that comes with pushing past your limits.

That feeling, that sense of accomplishment and pride, is what awaits you on the other side of your comfort zone. It's the reward for being brave enough to bet on yourself, even when the odds feel stacked against you.

The Resilience of the Human Spirit

I remember the pain of my divorce, the sense of failure and loss that consumed me. It was the lowest point in my life. It felt like my entire world had crumbled, and I didn't know how to pick up the pieces.

But here's the thing about rock bottom: it's solid ground. When you've hit the lowest point, there's nowhere to go but up. And that's when you discover the true resilience of the human spirit.

In those moments of darkness, when the self-doubt tries to become the loudest voice, you have a choice. You can either let it consume you, or you can open up your mouth and begin to speak positive words to yourself concerning your future and watching it come to pass.

I chose the latter. I decided that I wouldn't let my setbacks define me, that I would learn from them and come back stronger. And that's exactly what I did and so can you

With each failure, each moment of adversity, I gained a new perspective. I learned valuable lessons about myself, about life, and about what it takes to succeed. I discovered the strength within myself that I always desired would show itself.

And that's the beauty of the human spirit. It's unbreakable. No matter how many times we get knocked down, we have the power to rise again. We have the ability to transform our pain into purpose, our trials into triumphs.

So if you find yourself facing a seemingly insurmountable obstacle, remember this: you are stronger than you know. You have the resilience to weather any storm, to overcome any challenge. Believe in yourself, and trust in the power of God on the inside of you. .

The Importance of Faith and Purpose

Which would you rather have: success without fulfillment, or a life filled with meaning and purpose? It's a question worth pondering. What if I shared with you a way you could have all three; fit success, fulfillment, a life full of meaning and purpose?

For much of my early life, I chased trophies and medals. I wanted to prove myself, to show the world that I was the best player or the fastest runner; even the highest jumper. But as I achieved more and more, I realized that something was missing. I had the accolades, but I didn't have a sense of fulfillment.

It wasn't until a man named Author Moore, a former NFL player introduced me to my Lord and Savior, Jesus, that everything changed. Suddenly, my success had meaning. It wasn't just about me anymore; it was about the impact I could have on others, the legacy I could leave behind.

When you have a strong sense of purpose, when you believe in something bigger than yourself, it becomes a guiding light. It gives you direction and clarity, even in the face of self-doubt and adversity.

For me, that purpose is rooted in my faith in Christ. It's the belief that I was put on this earth for a reason, that my life has meaning beyond my own personal gains. It's the understanding that my journey, with all its ups and downs, is part of a greater plan.

And that faith, that sense of purpose, has carried me through some of the darkest moments of my life. It's been my anchor, my source of strength and resilience.

So if you're feeling lost, if you're searching for something more, I encourage you to take a step back and reflect on your own purpose. What drives you? What gives your life meaning? What legacy do you want to leave behind?

When you have a clear sense of purpose, when you're anchored in something greater than yourself, you'll find that self-doubt starts to lose its grip. You'll have a newfound resilience, a determination to keep pushing forward even when the road gets tough.

The Seven Keys to Fit Success

If there's one thing I've learned on my journey, it's that success leaves clues. There are certain principles, certain keys, that can unlock your potential and help you overcome self-doubt.

In my book, "The Seven Keys to Fit Success," I outline a framework for achieving your goals and becoming the best version of yourself. These keys have been a game changer for me, and I believe they can be for you too.

The first key is faith and positive self-talk. As I mentioned earlier, having faith in something greater than yourself, whether it's a higher power or a sense of purpose, can give you the strength and resilience to push through challenges.

The way you speak to yourself matters. When you become your own biggest cheerleader, when you replace negative thoughts with empowering affirmations, you become what you say and your ability to win becomes evident. .

The second key is patience and diligence. Success rarely happens overnight. It takes time, effort, and consistency. When you cultivate patience and diligence, when you trust the process and keep showing up even when results aren't immediate, you set yourself up for long-term success.

The third key is self-confidence. Believing in yourself is non-negotiable. When you have self-confidence, when you trust your abilities and your decision-making, you become unstoppable.

The fourth key is preparation. Success favors the

prepared. When you put in the work, when you educate yourself and develop your skills, you build a foundation of competence that can weather any storm.

The fifth key is having a good reputation. Your reputation precedes you. When you consistently show up as your best self, when you lead with integrity and excellence, doors start to open. People want to work with those they trust and respect.

The sixth key is having a mentor. You can achieve so much more, faster with a guide. When you have someone showing you how to avoid failure, it propels you to greater levels with fewer downfalls. A mentor is the counsel we need to help us along our fit success journey. Your mentor will be the one that allows you to remain humble, knowing that it was all your own efforts in reaching your fit dreams.

The seventh and final key is being a good money manager. Financial stability gives you options and peace of mind. When you're able to manage your money effectively, when you make smart financial decisions, you create a safety net that allows you to take calculated risks and pursue your dreams.

These seven keys have been instrumental in my own journey of overcoming self-doubt and achieving fit success. They provide a roadmap, a framework for personal growth and development.

And the beauty of these seven keys to fit success is that they're accessible to anyone. It doesn't matter where you come from or what obstacles you face. When you start implementing these principles in your own life, when you make them a part of your daily habits and mindset, you'll start to see incredible shifts.

The Ripple Effect of Believing in Yourself

Have you ever considered the impact that your own journey of self-belief can have on others? The way you show up in the world, the way you overcome challenges and pursue your dreams, has a ripple effect that extends far beyond yourself.

When I started believing in myself, when I started shattering my own self-doubts and limiting beliefs, I noticed something incredible happening. People around me started to believe in themselves too.

They saw the changes I was making, the success I was achieving, and it sparked something within them. They started to see possibilities where they once saw limitations. They started to dream bigger and take bolder actions.

And that's the thing about self-belief: it's contagious. When you have the courage to bet on yourself, to chase your dreams unapologetically, you give others permission to do the same.

You become a living example of what's possible when you refuse to let self-doubt hold you back. You inspire others to break free from their own mental chains and step into their greatness.

That's the legacy I want to leave. Not just one of personal success, but one of impact. I want my journey to be a catalyst for others to believe in themselves and pursue their own extraordinary lives.

Because at the end of the day, that's what it's all about. It's about using our own stories, our own triumphs over self-doubt, to light the way for others. It's about creating a ripple effect of positive change that touches lives and transforms communities.

So as you continue on your own journey of self-belief, remember that your story matters. Your victories over self-doubt, your perseverance in the face of challenges, have the power to inspire and impact others in ways you may never even know.

Embrace your role as a leader, as a trailblazer. Use your experiences to empower others and leave a legacy that extends far beyond your own personal achievements. Here's an additional leadership lesson I'll leave with you to ponder: At some point in your life you're going to have to set a goal that you think is impossible; and then you're going to have to do it. When you do it, your life will never be the same again. (Rich Thawley)

The Choice to Believe

As I reflect on my journey, on the battles I've fought against self-doubt and the victories I've claimed, there's one truth that stands out above all else: believing in yourself is a choice.

Every single day, we're faced with a decision. We can choose to listen to the voice of self-doubt, to let our fears and insecurities dictate our actions. Or we can choose to believe in ourselves, to trust in our abilities and our potential.

It's not always an easy choice. There will be moments when the doubts feel overwhelming, when the challenges seem insurmountable. But in those moments, we have to remind ourselves that we have the power to choose our perspective. Say to yourself in the mirror: Do you know who you are, I AM (put in your name) created in the image of God. I AM crafted and designed for greatness and because God lives in ME, I HAVE THE POWER to change MY circumstance, surrounding and MY environment.

We can choose to focus on our limitations, or we can choose to focus on our strengths. We can choose to dwell on our past failures, or we can choose to learn from them and keep moving forward. The Bible says it this way Proverbs 18:21.. Death and Life are in the power of the tongue; And those who love it will eat its fruits. I want you to choose to focus on your strengths.

When we make the conscious decision to believe in ourselves, to encourage ourselves even when others don't, something incredible happens. We start to show up differently in the world. We carry ourselves with a newfound confidence and resilience.

And that self-belief becomes a self-fulfilling

prophecy. When we believe we can achieve something, we're more likely to take the actions necessary to make it happen. We're more likely to persevere in the face of setbacks and keep pushing towards our goals.

So if you find yourself at a crossroads, if you're facing a decision that feels scary or uncertain, remember that you have the power to choose belief over doubt. Lean on my seven keys to fit success to help you get started. You have the power to reclaim your narrative and step into your greatness.

It won't always be easy, but it will always be worth it. Because when you believe in yourself, when you have the courage to bet on your own potential, you open up a world of possibilities.

You start to dream bigger, to take bolder risks, to pursue the life you truly want. You start to understand that self-doubt is just a temporary roadblock, not a permanent detour.

And as you continue to choose belief, as you continue to show up as the best version of yourself, you'll find that your capacity for greatness expands. You'll discover strength and resilience you never knew you had.

A Final Reminder for the Journey Ahead

I want to leave you with one final thought. A reminder to carry with you as you navigate your own journey of self-belief and personal growth.

Your doubts, your fears, your failures, nor your insecurities - they do not define you. They are not a reflection of your worth or your potential. They are simply a part of the human experience, a challenge that we all face at one point or another.

But you, my friend, are so much more than your doubts. You are a force to be reckoned with, a being of infinite potential. You have the power to shape your reality, to create a life that exceeds your wildest dreams.

So when those doubts try to creep in, when that voice of self-doubt starts to whisper in your ear, remember this and SAY: I AM enough. I AM worthy. I AM capable of extraordinary things.

Believe in yourself fiercely, unapologetically. Surround yourself with people who fuel your faith and challenge you to grow. Embrace the discomfort of stepping outside your comfort zone, knowing that that's where the magic happens and become HUNGRY for it!

And most importantly, never forget that your journey is your own. Don't compare yourself to others or try to fit into someone else's mold. Embrace your unique quirks, your strengths, your experiences. They are what make you special, what set you apart.

As you continue on this path of self-discovery and personal growth, know that I am cheering you on every step of the way. I believe in you and your ability to overcome any obstacle, to shatter any self-doubt.

So go forth with boldness and confidence, with resilience, with an unwavering belief in yourself. The world needs your light, your gifts, your unique contribution.

Embrace your greatness, and watch as your wildest dreams become your reality.

TrevisMichelle

TrevisMichelle, an accomplished author, award-winning speaker, divorce strategist, advocate, and cervical cancer conqueror, empowers women to build resilience by shifting their mindset when facing life's challenges. Her personal journey, overcoming trauma and cervical cancer inspired her to provide women with the tools and guidance to conquer those challenges one step at a time. She specializes in nurturing resilience, empowerment and confidence, and is dedicated to helping women become engaged participants in their life journey. A divorcee, TrevisMichelle is also a divorce strategist. She guides women through divorce with a step-by-step strategic plan, fostering resilience for healing while saving time and money and maintaining sanity. Her approach empowers women to find inner and outer fulfillment, and navigate the logistics of divorce for a new beginning.

By preparing ahead of time, gathering financial records, and assembling the right support team, women can navigate the divorce process with resilience, saving time and money and maintaining their sanity. She can be reached at www.trevismichelle.com

Chapter 12
"Gaining grace, resilience & confidence"

Trevis Michelle

trevismichelle

www.trevismichelle.com

GAINING GRACE, RESILIENCE AND CONFIDENCE

TREVISMICHELLE

Speaker, Best-Selling Author, Divorce Strategist and Podcast Host

In life, you've got to do what needs to be done. You've only got one life to live and you are the captain of your own destiny. It took me a long time to realize that.

Today, I am fortunate to be a best-selling author, inspirational speaker and advocate. My life's mission is to inspire, encourage and empower women to confront life's greatest challenges head on, while helping them build their resilience and confidence. I equip women with the tools they need to navigate their challenges with grace, resilience, and confidence, by showing them that personal transformation begins in the mind. Much of what I share with women today stems from my own personal experiences and challenges.

Growing up as a child, it's almost as if I lived in two worlds; my parents' world and my grandparents' world. These worlds were totally opposite from one another. When I lived with my parents, or just my mother, it was a world of abuse and attacks on my self-esteem and confidence. Neither one of my parents were loving or nurturing towards me. I had to tread lightly around my mother so that she would not take out her anger and daily frustrations on me.

She made it clear that her priority was keeping her man and that she would never let her child (me) interfere with that. My father did not try to protect me - it was easier to ignore me. He made the decision to help raise his girlfriend's two children that weren't even his; they were more important to him than me. My parents had their own issues with each other and a lot of the stress within their relationship got projected onto me. They told me that I didn't matter, that I wasn't important, and then their treatment of me backed up their words. It seemed as though my parents were more concerned with arguing with each other and not making me a priority. My parents divorced when I was nine years old.

When I was growing up, I also lived with my grandparents. They were both loving and nurturing toward me and showered me with love on a daily basis while living with them. They were my role models growing up. I had other role models who were influential in my life as well. In fact, one of them was Les Brown. Something he often said that struck a chord with me was that no matter what I was going through, I was great. My grandmother, Alice Pressley, would always tell me that I was great and that I would need to share my story one day.

"You have something special. You have greatness in you. You have the ability to do more than you can ever begin to imagine."

~ Les Brown

Another influential person in my life was Alice Walker, the author of "The Color Purple," who knew that Whoopi Goldber's character, Sealy, would be me later on as a teenager. My grandparents had a major influence on my life and I learned a lot from them. They had a relationship with God and made sure that I was exposed so that I could make my own choice to follow Him while growing up. I know I would not have survived without their love and guidance. They would make sure that I did well in school, and enrolled me into private school from Kindergarten through 7th grade. I was an only child at that time, so I would read a lot of books to escape the reality of having to go back to my Mother and deal with rejection and abuse.

The contrast between these two worlds, one of pure love and acceptance and the other one of anger and pain, made me believe that I was not important and definitely was not good enough to be loved. If they could not love me, why should anyone else? My grandparents reinforced the idea that I was enough and deserved to be loved, and that I had greatness within me, and that I would one day serve others in a positive way. I had come from love and as my grandmother would say, "good stock," so I should serve others. Through them, I understood that one of my greatest assets was my voice and my ability to communicate. They taught me that life was always going to have challenges, but the important thing was how you dealt with those challenges and that I would come through the difficult times with the help of God.

Living back and forth in these two very different worlds turned me into a people pleaser. I was always seeking acceptance and love. But I found it hard to gain acceptance from my peers because I did not use slang, did not dress in the current styles and was not allowed to play outside of my grandparents' fenced in yard. They went to public schools and I went to a private school, they had the latest clothes, they were part of a group. During the summer, they all hung out together at summer camp. My grandparents packed me up and took me to Europe during the summer so that I could become "cultured". I wound up spending a lot of time around adults and not enough time around kids my own age.

When I was in junior high and high school, I found it difficult to blend in with the "cool kids" because I was different. I was bullied because of my good grades, being a Northerner in a Southern state and because I spoke "proper." Fortunately, I became good at avoiding getting into fights because I would talk my way out of tense situations. It's a good thing because I couldn't fight to save my life. With all the reading I did, my vocabulary was extensive, which is one of the reasons they had a problem with me. I learned to use my book knowledge to keep me out of harm's way by tutoring and helping to write students' papers, and after a while, they left me alone, most of the time.

The way my mother and father treated me actually became a source of inspiration for me later on. I was determined to never treat my own children the way they treated me. I would always love them, even if times got tough, as I found myself going through my own divorce. My children would always come first and my love and support for them would never waiver. I would always reinforce how important and precious they were.

In high school, I wanted to be a lawyer or open heart surgeon because I wanted to make a difference in the lives of others. If I could not stand up for myself, at least I would stand up for others and be an inspiration so I would not repeat my parents' patterns of selfishness.

Growing up I would read book after book, sometimes two at a time. Reading allowed me to dream and escape the harsh realities of my life while living with my Mother. One of my favorite books was "I Know Why the Caged Bird Sings", by Maya Angelou. That book meant a lot to me. She was kind of a shero to me. Her poetry was also an inspiration, especially about digging deep and rising above my circumstances. When I read The Color Purple and then saw the movie, I would think to myself, If they can overcome, so can I. God, I know you have not left me and I do not blame you. Despite the traumas I have experienced, I know God has my back and I am a Conqueror!

Despite the traumas, I still had the desire to serve others and give back. My grandmother's voice was always in my head saying, "the best revenge is to succeed." I will show all of them that I am good enough and I will achieve my dreams.

So, that's where this desire to help other people who face challenges and are stuck in place believing that they cannot do better, and end up hurting others, stems from. I especially want to help men and women navigate through the divorce process so that they can live life on their own terms, healed and knowing they are good enough. If they have children, I emphasize to them that their child(ren) are also going through the divorce, as well as family, friends and co-workers. It's everyone you interact with in your community and daily life. I also emphasize that they are more than their divorce, this is a temporary situation.

The Stakes were High

Early in my life, the stakes were high. I refused to allow negativity to control me and my life. I couldn't let it invade my soul. I didn't want to repeat all of the same patterns my parents did, I knew I could and would do better. I just had to.

When my mom, brother and I moved to Florida, we left my grandparents back in New York. I was alone with no one to help me talk to or to help me escape the almost daily abuse. My physical safety at home and my physical safety at school was my priority, so my mental and emotional well-being suffered. I had to hold on fiercely to my grandparents' words of love and know that one day I would return back to them, my safe haven. I reminded myself daily that, as soon as I was an adult, I was going to escape, I would not give up....I could not give up. I was not and would not become a statistic. I remembered Les Brown's words. "If you fall on your back, and you can look up, then you can get up". I knew I might bend, but I was not going to break, I was going to get up and fight!

Things got really bad in Florida. I had to learn to survive in my own home. I developed my own survival strategies. I had a lot of anger, but I dare not show it because I knew I would put myself in danger. I buried my anger, my tears and my pain. Every day I wished I did not have to go home and that the bus would break down, anything to delay walking into that house. Every morning when leaving my home, I would breathe a sigh of relief, because it represented freedom, even though I had to be careful at school too.

I'd dream daily of running into my grandparents' open arms and feeling their warmth and love engulf me, washing all of my pain away. But my mother stood in my way. Even when they would call, she would sit next to me with the other phone in her hand listening and sometimes pinching me so hard to make sure I would not expose the abuse I was going through. I made sure to sound happy and express that everything was fine. I wrote letter after letter to them, begging them to come rescue me. They did not come, so I knew my mother was telling them lies and they had no way to know the difference. Years later, when going through my mother's papers after her death, I found the letters I had written. My mother had stolen them, so they were never even mailed. .

Due to trauma after trauma (physical, emotional, mental), one day I decided I would be better off dead. I attempted suicide by taking a bottle of pills, you see I read up on how much to take to get the job done. I just did not want to live in this hell anymore. Well, I did not succeed. My stomach was pumped, my mother and her boyfriend convinced the doctor that this was an accident and to let them take me back home. The doctor agreed and the abuse continued.

Since my suicide attempt failed, I realized I was supposed to live, God wanted me to live. I prayed so hard and I heard God say, "you are here for a reason, to share your story and give me glory." I made a conscious decision that day that I would fight, if not for me, for the baby I was carrying and to one day share my story..

> *"You were created on purpose for a purpose. There is a thirst and hunger in your heart that is real. Pay attention to it."*
> ~ *Les Brown*

Getting Help

Towards the end of my divorce, I started therapy. If it had not been for my children saying to me one day,

"Mommy why are you yelling at us," I may not have made this decision. I was yelling at them and making them feel unloved and taking my frustrations out on them. I had to take immediate action, no way was I going to let my babies feel the way I did. If it had not been for God, my grandparents and finding a good therapist, I would not be able to share my story from a position of conqueror and overcomer. I might have become a statistic and possibly hooked on drugs, alcohol and be a part of the street life. However, due to God's grace and my grandparents' planting a seed in good soil (me) and watering me through love and prayer, and me accepting Christ at an early age, I am still here and able to love and be loved. I do not blame God, instead I share my story to bring inspiration and hope to others. If I can overcome, so can you.

Concessions and Trade-Offs

I married a man who was considerably older than myself. At the time we got married, it wasn't about love at first. I was in survival mode, he made me feel safe and loved. It was more about security, and having someone that showed me love, besides I was more comfortable with older people having been raised partially by grandparents. Over time I grew to love him more and more. He was a good father. And he was loving toward me when we first dated and right after

we were married . He treated me like a queen. He told his friends that I was his "trophy wife". That was my first clue that he didn't take me seriously as an equal. He was very controlling. I was actually used to being told what to do by my mother, so it was easy for me to "fall in line.".

There was an unhealthy dynamic that developed in our relationship that I was in denial about for a long time. He was condescending toward me, which destroyed my self-esteem. I would make suggestions about something or voice my opinion and he would put me down or make fun of me. I allowed it to go on for so long that this became our standard way of communicating. His ideas and his way of thinking were superior to mine. That wasn't bad enough, he would also belittle me for my way of thinking and for voicing my opinions. At times, I was reluctant to communicate with him at all, wanting to protect myself emotionally from his put-downs. I remembered that my father used to treat me exactly the same way. I couldn't confront my father about it because I was a child and had to be seen and not heard. This made it easier for me to tolerate my husband treating me the same way, by not respecting my opinions and thoughts unless they were in agreement with his. I did not challenge him, I kept quiet. I allowed the behavior to continue for years. One day I said to myself, "I must bring this out in him, it is my fault."

For years, I rationalized it as a sort of trade-off. He's a good father and a good provider, so I just have to put up with this. I was hoping that, given enough time, he would grow to appreciate my intelligence and my opinions. I know it was insanity, experiencing the same thing over and over again, expecting a different outcome. I felt an obligation to be a good mom and a good wife in order to keep the marriage and the family together.

My husband and I went to church. I made sure children were in church too. We looked great on the outside, with the fur coats and the Volvo, and our vacations abroad. But on the inside, it was another reality. I was taught that you can't let people know what's going on inside your house, and you definitely can't let them know how you really think and feel because, due to past experiences, I know the consequences will be harsh. Survival mode dictates, "don't trust anyone". Meanwhile, all of this was slowly eating away at my self esteem and confidence, and I didn't even realize it. I didn't feel I was worthy or good enough. I couldn't be the best I could be because I was sacrificing myself for everyone else. I eventually came to realize that you can't do both at the same time.

Unfortunately, I didn't have much in the way of a support group or network. I attended some women's retreats that were organized by our church, but I never felt comfortable enough to open up. I felt that if I really did open up, I would fall apart at the seams. I was afraid that if I said something, people in my circle would react: "Girl, what's the matter with you? You got a great husband. He does this. He does that". But they couldn't see what was happening to me on the inside.

Part of the problem was that as I was growing up, I never had any really close girlfriends, so the process of sharing with a group of women was foreign to me and scary. The girlfriends I did have always ended up betraying me or being jealous of me, not knowing that I was envious of them. I was always on the outside of the group, looking in, hoping to be invited to the party.

I still had my grandparents, at least until my grandfather passed. At this stage of my life, it didn't feel right to unload all of my stuff onto my grandmother, Alice Pressley. Just the same, my grandmother always had my back, my front and both of my sides. She was my rock. She was a prayer warrior and she told me that she prayed for me from the time I was in my mother's belly, born and every day of my life. I didn't have any support from my own parents, so to a large extent I was really isolated.

I saw myself as a big failure. I was in that failure mode. And then I kept reinforcing it by believing it. My grandparents were together for more than fifty years, and here I can't make my marriage work. It was exhausting. It was debilitating. My heart was breaking because I could not hold the family together. I told myself that this must be my fault, since my husband was older and wiser, "what is wrong with me?" I thought he was guiding me, when in actuality he was molding me to be who he wanted, while also controlling me. As my unhappiness grew, I knew deep down inside that I still had a purpose and a reason to exist. I just didn't know what it was.

The dynamic in my marriage manifested as a personal, internal conflict. For some strange reason, I felt a sense of shame. I would tell myself that, "this isn't working for me, so it must be me. I'm the source of the problem". My parents' divorce conditioned me to think in terms of keeping the relationship together for the sake of the children and family stability, because I did not want my children to go through what I did. I put a lot of pressure on myself to make it work, fix it, try harder. I took a backseat, as usual because my self worth, self esteem and confidence were at an all time low.

It really wasn't a lack of confidence, it was that I was starting to feel unloved and not worthy or good enough. I would make sure to apologize and take the fault hoping he would be kinder. My people-pleasing skills were in full effect, I had had a lot of practice. I had to make my husband happy and my children happy, meanwhile no one was really happy. I did not want to disappoint my grandparents, I only wanted them to be proud of me. I was even still stuck on seeking love and approval from my mother and my father, who continued to treat me with disdain and were barely present for my children. I kept opening that door, only to have it shut in my face, again and again.

My grandmother was always supportive. She would say, "baby I am here for you. Life does not always work out the way you want it to, don't give up...I am still so proud of you." My grandmother's friends would say the same things to me, but I just didn't feel it and definitely did not believe it to be true. I was still in survival mode. That's all I knew. All I could do was pray; "God give me strength and please don't leave me".

One day, it hit me. Enough was enough. I decided to pursue a divorce. For once in my life, I needed to do something just for me. It felt awful. When I realized that it was time for me to walk away, I felt like such a failure. This was a low point in my life. I cried and cried, screamed into a pillow, snot everywhere. There comes a time when you realize if you don't make a move now, you will be stuck and die in that spot. Nope, not going to happen.

By this time, I was a stay-at-home mom, so I didn't have any income of my own and definitely could not pay an attorney. Time was of the essence because the verbal abuse was escalating, not always in front of the children. I was so ashamed, you see I was active in my church, my community organizations and everyone thought I had such a great life.

The Last Straw

I needed to follow my dreams, pursue a career so I could support myself and my children while still serving others, so I enrolled into a baccalaureate program to become a Registered Nurse. . This was an awakening experience for me, the start of new life, a new me. Here I was, surrounded by people from different cultural backgrounds, who listened and valued my opinions.

I felt intelligent again and the fire to do more than survive was starting up in my belly. World, watch out, I am on my way.

At the same time, things went from bad to worse at home. He was a good husband until he wasn't. The verbal and emotional abuse was becoming unbearable. He would wait until I was studying at 3am to start an argument, try to push my books away while I was reading, it was really ugly. On top of that, his infidelity became unbearable. How many times am I expected to forgive? Receiving threatening phone calls from his mistress, several times per week, enough is enough. I forgave for the last time. I was done. I deserved better, I wanted better. If I don't make a change, I'm sending the wrong message to my children that this kind of toxic relationship is acceptable. It would be much better for them to be raised separately and to have a mom who was healthy and happy. The divorce was difficult for them. Everybody suffers in a divorce.

Discovering Happiness Again

Going back to school made me happy. I loved getting up in the morning and going through my routine. I would drop the kids at school, and then off to class. It made me realize how much I had enjoyed school and enjoyed learning. Every day I was excited.

I had enrolled in college right after high school graduation, but when I became pregnant, I had to drop out of college and return to New York. I started to experience my love for reading, studying, and complaining about having to take tests. I was in heaven, and I felt like a kid again.

Nursing school is not easy though. The professors can be very tough on you. You have to study hard because it's all science; biology and chemistry, and there's a lot to learn and memorize. But I did what I had to do and got my As and Bs. Most of the students were much younger, but we studied together, encouraged and supported each other, regardless. I remember them saying, "you got this, join our study group." Those study groups were priceless, I know they helped me maintain my As and Bs. Being in college again, changed my whole outlook on my life. It gave me a break from my mom and wife role, since we were still living in the same household. I felt proud of myself again. "I'm TrevisMichelle. I am intelligent, I got this". I was the one who was going to walk across that stage to receive my degree in front of my children and my grandmother, Alice Pressley, graduate of Bethune Cookman College..

I still had negative and self-sabotaging thoughts to deal with though. I'm a nursing student who is going through a divorce and I'm broke. How am I going to do this? How could I possibly do this? But something deep down inside of me said, "You will do this, there is nothing too hard for God, keep moving." I kept hearing Les Brown and my grandmother, Alice Pressley telling me that I'm great.

One of my fellow students was a mother of four who was also going through a divorce. Our situations were similar. There were times when I had doubts and didn't think I would make it through, and she would say, "Snap out of it. You're doing this. We're going to do this together".

During this time, my mother, true to form, refused to lend any kind of support. I asked her for help and she said, "You and your children need to go into a shelter if you don't have any place to stay. You're not coming here". My mother lived in the upstairs apartment in my grandmother's house, and she was elderly. I knew I could not bring three children and a dog. My grandmother said, "Baby, I will pay for your attorney and help you financially." That fire in my belly was burning brighter, I was not alone, I had help. I could see freedom right in front of me. I kept putting one foot in front of the other with my blinders on and my ear muffs secured over my ears. My grandma used to say, "You cannot make progress walking forward if you're always looking backwards". So, I just kept looking and walking forward.

Don't look back!! Look ahead, move forward and make this your best year ever! You have that something special. You have GREATNESS within you!" ~ **Les Brown**

I didn't realize it at the time, but this was how my own method began. I call it the "W.A.L.K.(™) Method".

The first letter, 'W', stands for willing participant.

That's where transformation begins. You have to acknowledge that you need to make changes in your life, be willing to accept change and willing to do the work. Everything starts with the mindset shift. I understood that if my life was going to change, then I had to be willing to do what needed to be done to create that change, even if it looked daunting and even if it was painful.

The letter, 'A' stands for action. You must take action steps for change to occur. I had to find an attorney as one of my action steps. Some of those action steps for me were uncomfortable, saying that I wanted a divorce and then starting the divorce journey. My life was cushy on the outside, but it was painful on the inside.

The letter 'L' stands for love yourself by forgiving yourself. This one was the hardest step for me. I was always hard on myself, as were others and I had to forgive myself for failing as a wife and mother and granddaughter. Fortunately, my grandmother reminded me often that she loved me and supported my decision and would walk with me through the journey called divorce. This was a game changer for me, I had my grandmother in my corner. Loving myself had nothing to do with getting my hair and nails done. Loving myself was about forgiving me, Trevis Michelle. My grandma said, "baby girl, you have to forgive yourself". When I told her I was going through a divorce she said, "you know, baby, it's time. I support you. Forgive yourself for the role you played in that marriage." I couldn't put it all on him, even though I wanted to at times. I had to look at the role I played and do better and keep moving forward. Otherwise, it would have eaten me up inside and I wouldn't have been any good for my babies.

The letter 'K' stands for Kick butt unapologetically. When I realized I did not owe anyone an apology for putting my mental, emotional and physical health first, it freed me up to W.A.L.K.(™) in my power, one step at a time and dream big. I didn't realize this was my method until later on.

I attended a women's retreat through my church and they were surprised. Here I am, a mother in my thirties, and I'm going back to school to become a nurse? Some were impressed. Some of them would say something positive but then end by saying something negative. My grandmother used to call that a backhanded slap. I called my grandmother almost every single day. She was my cheerleader. Every day, she would remind me to put all my faith in God.

One of the teachers at my school learned about my divorce and she said, "I think while you're going through a divorce, you need to just put your schooling on the side for now and come back next semester or whenever you get through this. After you've gone through it, then come back because this is going to be too much for you".

So much for my own community supporting me

and believing in me. But I was used to that. All of that just turned up the fire inside of me. So, I increased my credits up to seventeen for the summer term. I had momentum and nothing was going to throw me off my track.

I still had the financial dilemma. All of our money was in joint bank accounts. But I had come to realize that I could make it on my own. Part of my husband's control over me was that he did not want me to work. He said, "I'll give you everything you need". And I just went along with it. But now, I needed to take responsibility and take back my power. I can work, get a job, be a mom and establish a career. I was in a nursing program that I loved, that would allow me to serve people and get paid well for doing it. I realized that I was the light in my own tunnel, I no longer had to look for it at the end of the tunnel. That fire was raging brightly.

Problem Solved and Then a New Problem

From the age of nine, when my parents went through their divorce, I began thinking about how the experience affected me in a negative way and how I would ensure that, no matter what, I would always let my children know that they were loved and appreciated and that they were special. I would never let them think that they were at fault and would try not to say anything negative about their father to them. So, I lived up to that. I reinforced in their minds that their father was a great dad. He just wasn't a good husband for me anymore.

I was able to move out, arrange housing and complete my degree. My children, my grandmother and even my mother were present when I walked across that stage and received my degree. That was a huge win for me.

I moved on with my life. Then, one day, I went in to see the doctor and heard these 5 words, "You have cervical cancer, curable." While everyone else heard death, I heard the word curable and became laser focused on overcoming this challenge. I thought to myself, "this is light work, you have been through worse and survived." After chemotherapy, external radiation and internal brachytherapy and surgery, I am still here and still standing by the grace of God, who declared "I shall live and not die."

Sometimes we take a few steps forward, then we find ourselves taking one or two steps back. This is a part of the process and journey called life. We are human and will make mistakes and get stuck, just don't stay stuck. Reach up, ask for help, accept it, and count all wins as a win. Your steps are stepping stones, so put one foot in front of the other and keep moving.

Show up for yourself and show the world who you are, you will be surprised who will give you a thumbs up, a clap on your back, a kind word to keep you moving forward toward your dreams, your greatness so that you can make an impact on the people around you and for you. One step leads to another step, it is called progress. Don't you dare give up!

Life is interesting, I had to go through the fire, fall down on my back, get up, bend and not break. This defined my W.A.L.K.(™) Method. I made a conscious decision to be a Willing participant, take Action, Love myself (forgive myself) and Kick butt unapologetically. My relationship and love of the Lord is stronger than ever because my grandparents, Alice & Clarence Pressley planted the seed and then watered me through love and prayer. My three adult children, Akil, Sasha & Kalik are my staunchest supporters. They know how much I love them and you know what, they love me back.

Today I am a cervical cancer conqueror, divorce survivor, divorce strategist, author & speaker, sharing my story with others and giving God the glory. Along this journey, I remind myself often that I am worthy, I am a conqueror, I am blessed and I have greatness inside of me.

"Dream bigger than your thoughts, and let your thoughts be bigger than your dreams."
~ TrevisMichelle

205

DR. JUANITA DANIELS-JOHNSON

Juanita Daniels-Johnson is the fifteenth child of Lena and Charles Daniels, who in total had 30 children, 19 of whom survived. Raised by her grandmother, Lonie Key Howard in Newark, NJ, she attended Sussex Avenue Elementary School and Arts High School. After graduation, she went to the Negro Ensemble Company to study Theatrical Arts in New York. Before completing her studies there she married Walt Johnson.

At nineteen she accompanied her husband as he traveled in the US Air Force. They have two daughters, Teresa and Kristen, but sadly lost their daughter Felicia through stillbirth. During their travels she has secured many licenses. Her educational experience includes a Colorado Teaching License, a BA in Organizational Leadership, an MA in Christian Education and a Doctorate in Christian Education. Currently she is a Colorado High School teacher.

She has also served as a pastor in many of the states they visited during the years of her husband's career in the military.

Chapter 13
"Juanita's journey: the sovereign hand of God"

🔾 pastorjuanitajohnson

Juanita's Journey: The Sovereign Hand of God

Dr. Juanita Daniels-Johnson

"And they overcame him by the blood of the lamb and the word of their testimony, and they did not love their lives to the death." Revelation 12:11 NKJV

"And thine ears shall hear a word behind thee, saying, this is the way, walk ye in it, when you turn to the right hand, and when ye turn to the left." Isaiah 30:21 KJV

This is my Testimony

You might remember the first time you felt truly loved. For me, that love came from my grandmother. Her name was Lonie Key Jones. She also carried the last name of Howard after her second marriage. I was raised by her because my mother bore so many children. Lena Mae Daniels was my mother's name, married to my father Charles Daniels. They say my mother bore thirty children in all, I always thought she should be in the Guinness book of World Records. Nineteen children lived. By the time I was born fourteen children were here already. One of my siblings died at two years old before I was born, her name was Darlene. Fearful that I would die also, my mother asked my grandmother if she would take me in and she did. My grandmother lived in more favorable circumstances than my parents. This would enable me to experience better opportunities. When I visited my parents' home, I did not feel comfortable. I felt more at home in my grandmother's house; after all, it was the home I really knew, loved and lived in. My mother never seemed to be glad to see me. As I grew older, I believed it was guilt coupled with her altered state caused by alcoholism.

GOD was there to give me the coping skills to overcome all of this. I called my grandma "Mama." She was also raising Carolyn and Emily, who were my older cousins. I felt like a rich kid in a mansion. The goodness of God provided them as helpers to Mama but also like servants to me. I must mention Miss Betty. She was my uncle's girlfriend; she was in charge of my hair. I loved Miss Betty. She was a tall, dark skinned lady who loved boiled noodles, chicken soup with hot sauce. She would place her hand on her hips and shake a tail feather. Emily had a voice like my mother Lena, it was a voice that sounded like opera. Emily discovered I could sing, and I could act. She provided opportunities for me to display my talents. Carolyn was the feisty sister. To me, she was beautiful, with beautiful legs, and she loved to listen to music. She would buy me beautiful things, and I learned how to be glamorous.

The First Whisper of Divine Love

My first experience with the Lord was at five years old. Imagine a moment when you felt something greater than yourself. I wanted to be on stage and took part in a production where I played Snow White. When I sang, I got a standing ovation because I could sing so well as a young child. That was the first time I really heard the voice of the Lord within my heart. I heard a voice that said, "Juanita, I love you." I said, "I love you too, God." From that moment, God became my first hero.

I felt a protection around me. Knowing that God loved me helped me endure the challenges I faced as a child. My family drank a lot on weekends, and there were often fights. But I knew I was loved, and that made me stronger. Performing became my outlet. By the time I was 13, I was given roles like Sister Margaret and Sister Odessa, where I had to preach out of the Book of Isaiah. The anointing and power I felt while preaching were undeniable.

A New Path: Love and Military Life

Which would you rather do: follow your dreams or follow your heart? In grammar school I learned to play the clarinet, and also played clarinet in the High School Band. I was preparing to go on to bigger and better things. My teacher, Mr Prestly Wood, saw my gifts and was determined to get me into the best high school, which was the Arts High School in Newark, New Jersey. You had to take a test to get in and I passed that test. He also continued to guide me until he was assured that my audition into the Negro Ensemble Company was successful. This was a school founded by

Douglas Turner Ward. I studied under James Moody, a renowned director and actor in the movies. It was a proud moment to attend that institution.

After graduating I met my husband who was also from New Jersey and had also been raised by his grandmother. He had dreams of joining the military, and my life began to shift focus. Going into the military with my husband was an escape from the potential pitfalls of alcoholism and drugs. In San Angelo, Texas, I tasted alcohol for the first time at 23 and loved it. Without spirituality in my life, I partied and drank hard for three years..

My husband and I traveled the world together, and while my acting and singing career took a backseat, I found ways to perform at summer festivals and within the communities where we were stationed. This world travel began to change me, exposing me to diverse cultures and people. It was during this time that I started to form deeper relationships with my siblings. It wasn't until I had another mystical experience with the Lord that things began to change.

God had been guiding me since I heard His voice at five. At 26, after losing my second daughter and having my third, God came into my life in a mysterious way. He had a plan, and His love was a constant sovereign force guiding me through my pain. My story of being sexually abused and how hard it was to forgive is a testament to that divine protection.

Challenges and Forgiveness: Finding Strength in Faith

Think about a time when you had to forgive someone who hurt you deeply. In a household filled with drinking and sometimes sexual abuse, I struggled to reconcile my feelings. I never had a relationship with my mother for many years, unable to understand why she gave me away but kept the other children. She had four more children after me and kept them. But through my experiences and God's guidance, I was able to forgive her and love her until the end.

Understanding her pain and her own traumatic experiences, including witnessing a rape, helped me to see her in a different light. My older siblings shared similar testimonies of not really knowing her, despite living in the same house.

When I lost my second daughter, Felicia Ann, it was a wake-up call. She was a stillborn, and though I never shed a tear, I knew it was God's mercy at work. I realized that it was now or never to get my story out. I had so many experiences and so much to teach and inspire others.

Teaching high schoolers about purpose became a new mission. Seeing young people without purpose and dealing with so much turmoil in the world, I wanted to let them know that there is hope. Sharing my victories and how God brought me through difficult times became a way to show them that they too can overcome.

Finding Purpose Through My Journey

Maybe you've faced a time when you knew you needed to change but felt powerless to do so. My struggle with alcohol was a difficult chapter in my life. Despite the love and support of my husband, I found myself drifting towards a path that was not meant for me. Drinking provided a temporary escape, but it also brought out a belligerent side of me. The anger that had been suppressed for so long came out violently when I drank.

Losing my second daughter, Felicia Ann, was the turning point. Despite her being stillborn, the calmness I felt through the ordeal was a clear message from God. It was His mercy at work, sparing me from a greater pain. This experience marked the beginning of my spiritual awakening. I realized that I needed to change, not just for myself but for my family and my relationship with God.

Think about a time when you found a new purpose in life. For me, it was when I decided to embrace spirituality and align my life with God's plan. My husband was a big part of this journey. Although he wasn't initially spiritual, I hoped that he would join me in my new path. However, I learned that change cannot be forced; it has to come from within.

I also felt pressure from the church. As a single woman in the church, I was often judged for my husband's absence. This added to my feelings of failure. But I learned that my relationship with God was personal, and it was not for others to judge. Over time, I understood that the spirit chooses us, and we cannot choose for others. This realization brought me peace.

Learning to Let Go and Trust in God's Timing

Can you remember a time when you had to let go and trust the process? One of the hardest lessons I learned was that I cannot change others; they have to choose to change themselves. This applied to my husband and later, to my children. My daughter, who initially resisted my guidance, eventually grew into a wonderful woman of God. This taught me that patience and faith are crucial.

I discovered that God's timing is perfect. It's not always in our timing that He wants to move. We must learn to watch and pray, trusting that He is working behind the scenes. This perspective changed how I approached life. I learned to pray for myself, not just for others, and to expect answers from God.

Prayer became an essential tool for facing challenges. Everything I did was prayed through. I prayed for guidance, for patience, and for strength. Joining Les Brown's team and sharing my story was a decision made through prayer. It brought excitement and a sense of purpose.

I realized that I didn't have to speak all the time.

Quietness became a virtue. Listening to others and letting the quietness teach me brought a new level of understanding. I began to see things differently, not just from my perspective but from a broader view. This growth was crucial in my journey.

Building Confidence and Overcoming Fear

For a long time, I procrastinated on writing my book, held back by fear and negative self-talk. But I realized that it was never too late to pursue my dreams. Working with Les Brown and his team built my confidence. Telling my story became a way to inspire others and to show them that God is always there, guiding us.

My husband's support was unwavering. He always provided for me, and I was what you would call a kept wife. His support allowed me to focus on my passions and to pursue my goals. I realized that my story, despite its challenges, was one of hope and divine intervention. God had always worked things out for me, and I wanted to share that with the world.

Losing my grandmother and my second daughter were two of the most significant losses in my life. My grandmother passed away at 97, and she was my hero. Her strength and wisdom were unparalleled. She chose to face death with dignity, refusing dialysis and staying in her right mind until the end. Her strength became a guiding light for me.

Losing Felicia Ann was another pivotal moment.

Despite the pain, I felt a calmness that I knew came from God. It was His way of protecting me from a greater suffering. This loss taught me about God's mercy and sovereignty. I knew that He was in charge, and His hand was over my life, guiding me through every challenge.

Realizing the Need for Change

At what point do we realize it's time to change? For me, it was when I saw the years passing by and knew I needed to change my thinking. If I wanted to make a difference in my life and the lives of my children, I had to act. I pursued education, earning my bachelor's, master's, and doctorate degrees. This journey was not just for me but to show my children and grandchildren that it's never too late to learn and grow.

I encouraged my grandson, Christopher Noah, to write a short children's book, showing him that creativity and learning are lifelong pursuits. Changing my approach meant being the change I wanted to see in my family. This legacy of education, creativity, and perseverance is what I want to leave behind.

Finding Serenity Through Spirituality

Think about a time when you found peace in something greater than yourself. My breakthrough came when I incorporated spirituality into my life. This new approach was different from everything else I had tried. It gave me a sense of serenity and purpose that nothing else could provide. I believe that the Creator wants His creation to know Him, and He has made Himself known to us in many ways.

You might remember the story of Genesis or Romans from the Bible, where God shows His love for us. This love became the cornerstone of my breakthrough. Even though we cannot see Him with the natural eye, He is always there. He is with us, guiding us, and showing Himself to us if we give Him a chance.

I approach the floor with my knees, reading scriptures and other inspirational works. This connection with God and other authors has been transformative. I look forward to the experiences and stories of others and how they will touch my story and make me a better person.

This method is different from everything else because it brings peace. Some people think that choosing a religion is a sign of weakness or a poverty mentality. But I know that the Lord is real. He is my friend, sticking closer than a brother. This realization has been my breakthrough, knowing that God wants what's best for me and that He wants my story told.

Embracing Success and Teaching the Next Generation

What are you if not a teacher to those who come after you? Success for me means feeling accomplished and self-actualized. Looking at Maslow's hierarchy of needs, I see that my needs have been met. Part of my self-actualization is writing and telling my story, speaking to others, and giving them the courage to speak up. This has increased my sense of purpose and fulfillment.

My life is different now because I can see the impact of my teachings on my children and grandchildren. I teach them about money, financial wisdom, and the importance of education. I hear my voice echoed in their teachings, which tells me that my efforts have not been in vain. Reaching my goals, like contributing to this book, brings a sense of relief and accomplishment.

How do you overcome negative self-talk? For me, it was about escaping doubt and fear. I had procrastinated for so long, held back by the belief that I would never tell my story. But now, I feel victorious. This journey has been about defeating negativity and embracing my purpose.

The Impact of New Insights on Others

How do your new insights affect those around you? My new insights have had a profound impact on my students and family. As a teacher, I provide a safe space for students to talk about their struggles, including their sexual identities. They know that as a pastor, I offer acceptance, love, and counsel. My daughter, who also teaches, often seeks my advice, and I guide her with kindness and wisdom.

My insights have taught me to look at situations from a positive standpoint, asking God what His plan is in every circumstance. Even in sickness and trials, I seek enlightenment. My cousin Emily, who helped raise me, is now 81 and very sick. I was able to encourage her, pray with her, and express my gratitude for all she did for me. These moments of connection and support are a testament to the impact of my new insights.

I want to leave a legacy for my children and grandchildren, not just in terms of material wealth but in the values and lessons I've imparted. My life mattered, and I want them to remember how I faced challenges and overcame them. This legacy of love, perseverance, and faith is what I want to pass on.

As I continue this journey, I am excited about the future and the opportunities to share my story. I've learned that it's never too late to change, to grow, and to inspire others. My breakthrough came through spirituality, prayer, and the realization that God's love is always there, guiding us.

A New Perspective: Learning to Watch and Pray

What are you if not patient? Over the years, I discovered that patience and prayer were key. Learning to watch as well as pray, I realized that my perspective was not the ultimate one. Understanding that God's timing is not always our timing was a significant lesson. Prayer became an integral part of my life, and I learned to expect answers and watch for them.

This change in perspective was transformative. I began to see things through a new lens, understanding that people are made in God's image and that we cannot change them. Only they can choose to change, and only God can guide them. This realization brought a sense of peace and acceptance into my life.

A Life Guided by Divine Love

What are your dreams, and how do you plan to achieve them? As I continue to share my story, I feel a renewed sense of purpose. I want to tell people about God's great love and how He is always close to us, directing our path. Teaching high schoolers about purpose and hope has become a mission for me. I want them to know that there is always hope, no matter how difficult the circumstances.

I'm excited about the future and where this journey will take me. I'm ready to serve, love, and learn. My perspective has changed, and I see things differently now. I've learned that quietness is a virtue and that listening is just as important as speaking.

Reflect on your own journey and the moments of divine guidance you've experienced. My life has been a testament to God's unique plan for each of us. From my grandmother's loving care to the challenges I faced and overcame, His hand has always been guiding me. I never knew a day of my mother's love, but I love her and honor her name. This journey has been about glorifying the Name of the LORD and sharing His love with others.

As I look back, I see how every moment, every

challenge, and every victory was part of His plan. My story is one of hope, resilience, and divine love. And as I move forward, I am excited to continue sharing this story, inspiring others, and embracing the future with faith and purpose.

NICOLE NABORS

Nicole Nabors is a licensed master social worker, and has a Master of Theology. She has Bachelors degree in philosophy & religion and psychology. Nicole works as a clinical therapist at the private practice she founded, Grace & Peace Counseling.

Nicole is a speaker and teacher who captivates audiences with transparency and vulnerability that inspires. She is the author of Dance Again: A Journey of Healing. Nicole is utilizing her skills to help the people who systemic programs fail to reach. Her goal is to bring light where there is darkness, love where there is hate, joy where there is sorrow, and peace where there is pain. She believes we cannot control what happens to us, but we can help one another to make things easier and more pleasant in this life.

Chapter 14
"Riding the storms of life
with grit and grace"

Nicole Nabors

nicole_nabors_9

www.nicolenabors.com

CHAPTER XIV

RIDING THE STORMS OF LIFE WITH GRIT AND GRACE

NICOLE NABORS

I was a curious kid, always on the lookout for the next big adventure. You could find me tagging along with the neighborhood boys, not because there weren't any girls around, but because I craved the excitement and the physical challenges they were up for. Climbing trees, racing bikes, playing basketball, you name it—I was all in

We all had our childhood heroes, right? My grandmothers were mine. They were these incredible women who seemed to have a direct line to wisdom. My maternal grandma could captivate an entire church with her prayers, while my paternal grandma used her healing hands as a nurse to make a difference. They were like superheroes without capes, and I'd listen, wide-eyed, soaking up every wise word. Who are the heroes in your life? What makes them special to you?

Then, there was that time I watched the movie "Sarafina" about the struggles of apartheid South Africa. It was a lightbulb moment—I knew I wanted to be a change-maker, someone who stood strong against unfairness and fought for what was right. That movie planted a seed that grew into my calling as a social worker. I was inspired by the courage of those like Angela Davis and the Black Panther Party.

223

I've always been the kind of person who watches and learns. Observing how people handle their feelings taught me a lot about life. Think about it, 80% of communication is nonverbal. Think about how you react when you're mad, sad, or over-the-moon happy. What does it take to bring a smile to your face? Each of these responses we communicate in our actions and deeds.

Being the eldest of three kids, I felt the pressure to set a good example—to be a beacon of hope amid our family's challenges. I did my best to guide my sister and my brother. It's like being the captain of a team, leading by example.

The Battle for Survival

Have you ever felt like you just didn't fit in? Like no matter what you did, it just wasn't quite right? I've been there. Growing up, I had to face a lot of rejection and learned some tough lessons about self-acceptance.

You see, my family was comfortable—we had enough to eat, and we never worried about the lights going off. But that didn't stop the teasing. Kids would make fun of my hair, my skin complexion, and even the gap between my teeth! I was just a girl trying to be myself, but that seemed to be everyone's problem.

When it feels like the world is pointing out all the ways you're different, it's tough. It took me a long time to look in the mirror and say, "Hey, I am enough, and

I'm okay just the way I am,." I had to believe that I was created with care and purpose, that nothing about me was a mistake.

Life threw me some curveballs, too. When I was just 15, my world got turned upside down. I lost someone I thought to be the love of my life—he was shot and killed. Around the same time, my parents split up after 23 years. It felt like everything that could go wrong, did.

But there was this little voice inside of me, a whisper really, that kept saying, "You're here to help others." So, I did just that. Helped out at the store, was a friend to a lonely stranger, and lent an ear to those who needed it. It wasn't easy, but it gave me a sense of purpose.

Now, I won't lie—it wasn't an overnight miracle. There were days I felt totally alone, even abandoned by God. And that was scary because my faith was my rock. Life wasn't done with the curveballs yet, a destructive storm came over my life a couple of years later.

It was September 9, 2006, and I was hanging out at my cousin's place. I knew she was in an abusive relationship at the time, but I didn't know the extent. Her boyfriend came over that day, and the next thing I knew, he pulled out a gun. He cocked it, walked up to my cousin who was laying on the floor, and said "If you ain't gonna be with me, you ain't gonna be nobody." He shot her three times in the head. I'll never forget the horrific image of him killing her point blank.

Then, he turned the gun on me. I did the only thing I could think of—I lifted my arms, I looked over his head and cried out loud, "Jesus, have mercy on me!" I kept calling out to Jesus, and he kept firing until, finally, the gun was empty and he ran out of the house.

When I woke up, I was in a hospital in a different city. When I woke up my family was there, but the doctors had nothing but bad news. I had been shot in my leg, torso, and neck. The bullet that entered my torso caused paralysis due to the damage of the spinal cord. I was in so much pain. It felt like every time they walked in, something else was wrong. I understood the language they used—I'd always wanted to be a doctor, and I had read a lot of medical books before. The things they were telling me… it was just too much. I was only 24 years old and my dreams felt like they were slipping away.

The Mirror's Reflection: Facing the Truth

Have you ever faced something so tough that it felt like you couldn't go on? How did you deal with it? I learned that it's not about what happens to us, but how we respond to it.

I had always been an athlete. I loved to run and play basketball. But now, my own body was like a stranger to me. It wouldn't do what I needed it to do, and it felt like even my body was rejecting me.

Feeling like a victim, facing rejection, hurt, and

abuse—it's heavy stuff to carry. Looking back now, I had always been stuck in a cycle of being selfish, prideful, and conceited as a protective layer to mask the hurt of not being enough. I was not a nice person. I was living in a façade, trying to convince myself I was okay, that I was happy.

You know that little voice that says, "You're not enough, you don't deserve good things, you're not lovable," I've heard it too. Sometimes, I'd ask God why certain things happened to me, why I wasn't protected. That voice would creep in again, "You're not enough."

Addiction runs in my family, and if I hadn't decided to change, I might've ended up on a similar path—stuck in sadness and not caring about anything. Trying to find love in all the wrong places could've trapped me in the same cycle. The same chains that held my family back for so long.

Did you know some people don't even realize they're stuck in a cycle? It's like they can't see the patterns they're repeating. But we can be the ones to see it and change it, what a gift.

In hindsight, it was all meant to happen this way. Here came a time when life gave me a major wake-up call, and I had no choice but to listen. All the ways I used to dodge my feelings—partying, smoking, it all just stopped working for me. I had to face the music and look myself in the mirror. And you know what? I didn't like what I saw. I had built myself up to be someone I wasn't, and I didn't even know who the real me was anymore.

But when everything else was stripped away, it was like an alarm ringing in my head. I was in the biggest fight of my life, and with God's help, I managed to come out on top. That tough time? It was actually the help I needed to start changing.

Regaining Control One Step at a Time

You see, when I got shot, it wasn't just my life that changed—it was like a shockwave hit my whole family. Everything was different, even the way we looked in family photos. It was tough on everyone, especially my little brother and sister, who had always seen me as their strong big sister.

A couple of weeks after the shooting, when I was moved to the surgical unit from the ICU, my siblings came to visit. That's when I had to tell them what had happened, and it was like I'd told the story a million times before. But this time, something cracked, and I started to cry. It was the first time I'd let the tears out since everything went down.

My brother was sitting right there at the end of my bed. And when he saw me cry, I'll never forget the look on his face. He was so shocked; that he had to leave the room. Later, he told me that he could only remember seeing me cry maybe twice in our whole lives. Seeing me like that was tough for him, but you know what? It brought us closer. It showed them that it's okay to be vulnerable, to be real with each other.

Now, if I'm being honest, there were times when I felt like giving up. But then I'd look at my little brother and sister, and they were like my last straw of hope. They were always looking up to me, and I knew I had to be strong for them. I wanted to show them that quitting just isn't what we do—it's not in our blood. Our granny faced a lot of tough stuff in her life, and she never gave up. We're cut from the same cloth; we were not made to quit.

Every time I encouraged them, I was really giving myself a pep talk too. "Keep going," I'd say, "even when it's hard, even if you feel alone, or like you're not enough." Because here's the thing: I survived. I made it out of that house, off that couch. The guy who shot me, he emptied his gun just three feet away, and somehow, he missed more than he should have. The cops found bullets all over the house, thinking that I was a moving target. But I wasn't and I'm still here, still breathing. It was like something else was watching over me.

I got really tired of feeling sorry for myself. I remembered how much I loved to laugh, to learn, to read. So, while I was getting better in the nursing home, I made a deal with myself to read a book every week. They were mostly about getting stronger in spirit and mind—nonfiction, self-help stuff, you know? It was like feeding my brain with the good stuff.

Instead of focusing on what I couldn't do, I started paying attention to what I could do. Even if it was something as simple as brushing my teeth—because that's what I could control. People were still helping me with basic needs, but I took back my power in the little things, like washing my face and brushing my teeth. And the more I used my mind, the more I started to think about what I could do with the abilities I still had. That's when the real journey began.

After the nursing home, I moved in with this guy named David, who'd been in a wheelchair for nearly ten years. His place was fully accessible, and it was in this quiet suburban area—perfect for getting myself together. David was this cool dude who didn't let anything stop him. He cooked, cleaned, mowed the lawn, and even threw great barbecues. Living with him, I started to try all sorts of new things, like wheelchair basketball and adaptive rock climbing. But kayaking? That's my slice of heaven—my Sanctuary Saturday morning.

I can confidently say David changed my life. Watching David showed me that I could still be an athlete, and that I could still live a full and active life. He inspired me to see things differently. Imagine if I had just gone back to my old apartment after the nursing home. I wouldn't have learned half the things I did from David. He didn't wait around for services to help him; he did everything himself.

The Healing Journey

I'm convinced that every single day I wake up, there's a reason for it. I'm here to make a difference, to shake things up for the better wherever I go. That could be with people I work with, my friends, my family, or even someone I've just met. I like to think of myself as a game changer, transforming the vibe of a place just by stepping foot in it.

I've climbed over so many obstacles that it's nothing short of a miracle I'm still around. Being here is proof that there's something bigger at play. Deep down, I've got this power to spark change. My mission is to figure out what my gifts are and move in sync with God's plan, so I can bring those gifts to life here on Earth with real impact. It's about my surroundings, my job, my calling, my purpose, and the special touch I've been given.

Without all these challenges, I never would've found my way to healing from the inside—making peace with my past, and forgiving myself and others. I've learned so much about who I am, and that journey never stops. If I hadn't gone through these tough times, I wouldn't be able to guide others on their path, to encourage and inspire them to find their way. Otherwise, I'd just be stuck running in circles, not even realizing I'm going nowhere, trapped by my own limits.

I used to think I wasn't enough—because of where I came from, because I'm a woman, you name it. I didn't think I was worthy or valuable. But guess what? I fought through those thoughts with therapy, lots of prayer, and a whole bunch of self-love. Instead of waiting for someone else to love me, I started treating myself right. I accepted everything that makes me ME!

It took forever for me to find my voice, to accept who I am, and to realize I'm perfectly made. That hurdle was massive, and I'm still jumping over it. I'm constantly reminding myself—little Nikki, don't stress. You're enough, you're loved, you're beautiful. I'm always cheering on the younger me because she's still healing.

I had to take on the war going on in my mind, all those automatic thoughts from past trauma. My brain was just trying to get by, but I had to switch gears and be my own cheerleader instead of my own critic.

I started to be careful about what I let in—what I listened to, what I watched, and even who I hung out with. I didn't want anything or anyone to make me doubt my worth. I made playlists full of tunes that lifted me up and got an app to send me reminders all day long about self-acceptance, self-love, and self-forgiveness. I'd say these affirmations out loud, really believing them.

Every night, I'd look in the mirror and tell myself three things I did well that day and three things I forgave myself for. I was building a whole new relationship with myself, knocking down those old lies that said I wasn't lovable or good enough. Sticking with this routine changed everything for me. Now, I don't need to act all proud or conceited because I'm truly confident in who I am. And real confidence? It doesn't need to make a scene. It's just a quiet knowing, being sure of myself, and my abilities, and trusting that I've got what it takes to handle whatever comes my way.

The Role of Faith in Overcoming Adversity

If you met me when I was 24, you'd hardly recognize me now. These days, nothing outside of me shakes me up—not even when I bump into something that used to unsettle me. I've learned to deal with it all. Life throws curveballs, but now I can handle them like a grown-up who's got her act together. Back in the day, life's storms used to knock me over and I'd be a total mess. Now? I surf those waves. I talk to the storm, telling it how it's going to be and how long they're allowed to stick around. And if they don't listen? No biggie—I love the thrill of the ride anyway.

It's kind of funny, actually. When I was in the Navy, I'd strap myself to the catwalk on the aircraft carrier and just lie there, watching the storms roll by. I'd get totally soaked, but man, did I enjoy it. Talk about coming full circle, huh?

Now, I won't lie to you—there were plenty of times I felt like giving up. But it seemed like God had other plans, scooping me up and keeping me moving even when I thought I was done for. I'd feel His strength when I had none, and suddenly, I'd be back on my feet, ready to take on the world again. People look at me and see strength, but what they don't know is that it's all thanks to God's grace.

There's this quote I love from the Bible, in Romans 8:18, that says, "For I reckon that the sufferings of this present time are not worthy to be compared with the glory which shall be revealed in us." That's like saying all the rough patches we go through don't even measure up to the amazing things within us, at our core—Strength, resilience, perseverance, dreams, hope, love, and purpose. It's these things that get us through the storms, and help us overcome our suffering. People might see me now, with my own business and as an author, and think it's all been smooth sailing. They don't see the tough times, the sleepless nights, and the tears. But all that hardship? It's just paving the way for the good stuff—the glory.

I think in some ways, we're all shaped by the people around us. I grew up with folks who were all about helping others. Both my grandmas were helpers—one with her faith and the other in healthcare. My dad was a minister who also worked in law enforcement, and my mom was in healthcare, too. Even my mother's sisters are in healthcare and my great aunts are nurses. So, for me, making a difference feels like it's all about giving a hand without expecting anything back. Just doing the right thing because it's the right thing.

Now that I'm a clinician myself, all those tough times and battles with myself help me be more patient and understanding with my clients, no matter where they're at. I get what it's like to struggle, to wrestle with your own thoughts and feelings. It makes me a better helper. People tell me I inspire them, that I'm strong and wise beyond my years.

Have you ever felt like you were in over your head, like the world was spinning too fast? I'm here to tell you, it's okay to feel that way. But remember, just like I learned to ride those storms, you can too. It might take some time, but you've got more strength inside you than you realize. And who knows? Maybe one day, you'll be the one inspiring others with your story. Keep pushing, keep growing, and most of all, keep being awesome. Ride the storms as they come!

Dr. Dwight S. Riddick, II

Dr. Dwight Riddick is a global speaker specializing in leadership development and working with organizations and individuals on the brink of giving up and looking to scale up while helping them maximize their potential. Dr. Riddick brings over 23 years of organizational leadership, 10+ years of executive coaching, serving as an adjunct professor, and on multiple community boards to execute social impact

Dr. Riddick's proven track record and expertise are used in his speaking to produce results by providing practical steps to transform the mindset and create predictable outcomes. He has earned certifications as a life coach with John Maxwell and trained with Eric "ET" Thomas and Jeremy Anderson. Dr. Riddick has been married for more than 16 years to Dr. Jennell Whitfield Riddick. They have a teenage son who is a national soccer player and an elementary-age skate sensation daughter. He lives to maximize the potential of others.

Chapter 15
"You are still here,
so make it happen"

 Dwight Shawrod Riddick

 dsriddick2

 www.dsriddick.com

CHAPTER XV

YOU ARE STILL HERE, SO MAKE IT HAPPEN: LIVE THE LIFE YOU WERE BORN TO LIVE.

DR. DWIGHT RIDDICK, II

I hope you are ready to buckle up for a chapter in my life—a stretch where I allowed procrastination, hesitation and seeming rejection to be unwelcome guests, permitting shame and guilt to snatch away the joy of living the life I was destined for. Looking back, I have realized that my journey would have taken a different path had I acted differently. In some cases life would have felt different if I had responded with a different perspective. I found myself unfairly condemning and beating up an innocent person—the one who made those choices no longer lives here. The real me survived and, like one of my favorite stories, I am the better version of my old self that lived to tell the story. Although everything around me seemed to cave in and be reduced to nothing, I am still here and am now living the life I was born to live.

You may wonder what exactly happened? Well, I grew up in a pretty decent home. My parents struggled when I was young and kept moving from house to apartment, and back into low-income areas again, but that did not last long. Eventually they both got on their feet and our family became well-off. My father acquired two doctoral degrees while my mother held a top position at a national college. They pushed me to do better and achieve higher levels of overall success. I wanted to be like them both. They inspired me, so I went after lofty goals. I was excelling in academics while also being recruited to play division 1 basketball. I was almost living a dream. I was our high school's basketball team captain, voted most likely to succeed, and chosen as prom king. It was really a movie. I had very high self-esteem, loved helping others who did not have access to what I thought was basic living, developed a plan for success, and set very high expectations of moving to the next level. I had not achieved grand success yet, but the potential was there. What I did not know was that my next nine years would bring a tremendous shift in what was normal. I had no idea that all of this blissful living would come tumbling down... and tumbling down it did come. I was living a Charles Dickens story, with both the best of times and worst of times all at once.

Acknowledge challenges to overcome

I was recruited to play on that division one basketball team and attended James Madison University which was the school of my dreams. However, the coach I went to play with was fired and so I too was given a decision to go away with him or stay and try out for the team with the incoming coach. I was sure I would make the team, so I stayed. As you can probably guess, I did not make the team. He cut me without hesitation.

This was extremely heartbreaking. It was not hard to handle like some young kid with hoop dreams, but it was more like a deep devastation to me as I felt like a hometown hero who was expected to be great at everything, and I had failed.

Today I am not even sure if the expectations were real, but I definitely thought they were. As a result, it was not even that I was cut from the team that tore me apart, it was not being valued, not being seen, and the idea of disappointing so many who had cheered me on and supported me. I later attempted to join a fraternity. It was to take a semester to complete the initiation process, but four semesters later I still had not crossed the burning sands into the fraternity. Then there was the issue of the 4-year education I went to acquire, as I found myself, 9 agonizing years into it, with no diploma and classes still to complete. This entire decade of my most formative years was excruciating.

To not accomplish any of this would make me a failure. It caused me to feel insignificant, incapable, and incompetent. It was the worst feeling I ever had. I started to treat other people rudely, and I avoided the people I loved. I volunteered to be homeless. I slept in the back of my truck in hotel and hospital parking lots instead of going home because shame had become the outfit I wore every day. These were just a few of the life delays that I experienced causing me to hit a low that I thought was inescapable. The weight of it all was seemingly unbearable. It created a fear that paralyzed me and a sense of guilt that kept me from believing I deserved anything greater.

Perhaps you, like me, have had major milestones in your life closely in sight and then all of sudden put on pause. Maybe you have lived in the emotional cave of despair and depression. I'm sure you have had dreams that seemed touchable for a moment but just out of reach. Like a child on their tiptoes reaching for an elusive balloon, you have been swiping at success only to watch it float away. You can most likely agree that, in this moment of life right now, you are experiencing the pain of having postponed something pivotal, or you are gazing into the rearview of life and contemplating what might have been. Unfortunately, time machines are not at our disposal, but what we do possess is the present moment. We stand here, breathing, with an opportunity to seize and maximize our lives. It's time to bid farewell to guilt and shame, to liberate ourselves from their burdens, and to fully embrace the life that awaits us. Say bye to that old self and throw a welcome party for who you are now.

Every day, we wake up with a chance to leave our mark on the world. The only ones exempt from this opportunity are those who have taken their final rest. But guess what? We're not in that category. So, let go of the past, release the weight of guilt and shame, and step into the abundance of possibilities that exist for you right now.

In the words of Al Williams, "All you can do is all you can do, and all you can do is enough." Make certain that you do everything within your power. I employ you to embark on this journey with me. Cease the self-flagellation; the past cannot be rewritten. Instead, pay it forward. Declare your intentions, take a stand, and commit to cultivating the gift of the present moment. I have heard it said that "yesterday is history, tomorrow is a mystery, but today is a gift and that's why they call it - the present". Open your present and maximize your potential.

Life unfolds in its own rhythm, and every experience, every trial, has sculpted me into the person I am today. I had to release fear, guilt, and shame to unveil the true essence of who I am meant to be. Embrace the concept that everything transpires in its due time. My experiences have forged the man you are meeting through these pages today, and this is my narrative—one I stand by. So yes, I was in undergrad for 9 years, but I did graduate. Not only from undergraduate, but also with a master's degree, and a doctoral degree, then several niche certifications. I tried out for the team again, and I made the team and became a lettered athlete at the division 1 level in the NCAA. Might I also add that I eventually joined the fraternity. While it was not in the same time frame as most, it was definitely right on time for me. What am I saying? I am saying that just because the first shots did not score, it did not mean that I could not win at the game of life. Although

I did not pass every class the first time, it did not mean I would not graduate to the next level of living. Yes, there was a moment that crossing the burning sands into a fraternity felt more like quick sand, but like Maya Angelou, Still I rise.

Lessons learned

If it happened for me, it can happen for you too. I have advised myself to stop waiting to see what else is going to happen and instead decide what I want life to be and then make it happen. I offer you that same advice. Take another shot. Enroll in another class. Pursue your destiny. We can achieve more if we get up from the floor and keep moving.

So, as we move forward, let's collectively extract the essence of life, banish fear, get rid of guilt, silence shame, and embrace the opportunities that surround us. It's time to milk every moment, savor every drop, and live authentically. This is our chance to define our story, and I invite you to join me on this incredible journey.

If you are wondering where to begin, let me share a few practical ways that I used to be able to start impacting life and not allow life to impact me. I decided that, like a jet fighter on an aircraft carrier, I would not just keep floating along and going where I was being towed, but instead I would fly. Yes, just like I was meant to do, I would fly. I would jump in the cockpit of confidence, turn on the engines of empowerment and take off to fly. It was that simple F.L.Y. - Focus Forward, Lean back into learning, and say Yes to my turn.

Focus forward

I began by focusing forward. I put into practice what I once read the author Paul of Tarsus say, "forget those things behind me, I press towards the mark..." I decided that my rearview was not going to ruin my front voyage into the unknown. I even created visuals to keep me focused. I purchased an alumni T-shirt and placed it on my dorm room wall even though I had not earned it yet. I borrowed some money and purchased a diploma frame and placed a one-hundred-dollar bill in it. Then I challenged myself to replace the hundred-dollar bill with a diploma within 2 years upon graduation. I went to the gym every day wearing official basketball gear from our school bookstore until I would officially receive the authentic gear from the coach to wear with the university's varsity team. I literally created visuals to help me stay focused on what I had not achieved yet. I believed, built it and as a result was able to see it.

What can you put in your view to help give value to where you are going? What could you write on a sticky note or hang up as a poster? What do you see yourself becoming despite what you have been? Where will you be in 6 months or next year without staying stuck where you have come from? Why keep riding in reverse when your vehicle to success has 5 or more gears to move you swiftly forward. When I focused forward it made it easier to forget what was behind. It allowed me to experience a newness of life that I had never felt before. The way up was to start flying by focusing forward. Now choose today to turn around and refocus. Forward is the direction your compass is leading you. Resist distractions that could waste your time. Unhitch from the emotions of fear, doubt, and resentment that wear you down and slow your pace. Focus forward and decide to fly.

Lean into learning

Next, I realized that to F.L.Y. I would have to lean into learning. By lean into, I mean learn to relax and gain new information instead of forcing my situation to fit my old way of thinking. Go forward with a blank-slate mentality. Once I released my anxiety, and concluded that every moment was an opportunity for growth I was free to soar. John Maxwell once said, "Sometimes you win, sometimes you learn." That was different for me, as I was used to either winning or losing. However, once I started turning what I thought were loses into learning moments the sky was now wide open to fly into it.

To be clear I did have to do a lot of unlearning, in order to lean into learning, but it was worth it. I untethered from bad habits, released some thoughts that I lived by as absolute truths, and humbled myself to a point of living without excessive luxury in order to exhaust value in what I had. I learned how to depend on others to help me, without becoming dependent only upon others. I learned that borrowing was not bad if, in fact, it helped me get ahead until I could return what I was loaned. Most of all I learned that I did not know what I did not know. There was a day where I was spent out of money but needed gas and a stranger at the gas pump was handing out gas cards on behalf of their church. It had to be divine timing, because there was no way the guy could have known that I pulled up to the tank with no money. Initially my pride kept me from accepting his offer. Then I realized that there had to be something bigger than me happening because without his help I would have been stranded. In that moment I learned that aid from others was not a sign of weakness, but in fact it was a show of strength. It took everything in me to muster up the ability to accept what was being offered.

Moments like these taught me lessons that not even 9 years of study would have explained to me. The process was more about revealing who I could become than it was about what was being revealed around me. I had the ability to be stretched. If I was flexible, I was unbreakable. These lessons I learned are not exclusive to me, they are universal and can be a part of your learning as well. Consider how much you have gained in information and ability during the most delayed seasons of your life. Write down the ways that you have been forced to design a new plan in order to thrive. You have learned that chaos gives birth to creativity. Now you can use creativity as proof that you are an inventor of positive results and alternative strategies even during your struggle. You too have leaned back into learning. The key is now to recognize that learning, not losing what has happened. When you shift your perspective and gaze at your future through the lens of learning, there is no more loss of identity, losing in life, rejection or delay. It all becomes a step on your staircase towards the cockpit of your jet headed towards achievement. You lean back, turn on the thrusters of learning and takeoff, to fly in the life you were destined to live.

Yes to your turn

Finally, I was able to really take off when I unleashed a, "Yes!" to my turn. That's right. After hearing, "no.", "not yet" "we chose someone else", and "you will have to wait", I finally decided to shout "Yes" to my turn. This is the simple practice of self-affirmation. It is more than visualization by placing items in your environment that you can see. This is digging deep within yourself and finding something positive that you can say. Your words are worth a thousand pictures, and can paint in hues of, "make it happen." What you say will often determine what you see. One of my favorite books says, "you have the power to speak those things that are not as though they already are." While I was dealing with my delay, I figured out that it could not always be someone

YOU ARE STILL HERE, SO MAKE IT HAPPEN

else's time to succeed and never mine. Eventually my time to succeed had to come. If my time was going to come, I could not keep waiting for someone else to give me permission to experience it, I had to decide that for myself. Jeff Lerner said, "If it's going to be, it's up to me." I heard that and I believed in it so much that I literally said aloud, "Yes!". Yes, I am going to make the team, yes, I am going to get into the fraternity, yes, I am going to graduate, and yes, I am going to fly and not stay grounded when I know there is more in me to accomplish and more people for me to serve.

I invested a little money and attended an online seminar hosted by Grant Cardone and the guest speaker was a Mary Kay top sales rep named Gloria Mayfield Banks. She mounted the stage with short natural hair, brown skin and an all white business outfit. She had a lot of energy and a huge smile. She began her presentation by saying, "If you are going to be successful you need to be loud about it, otherwise you cannot make it happen." Then she quoted what sounded like a poem that ended in her saying, "I am proud to be top rank, I am an elite national executive, my name is Gloria Mayfield Banks! That's how I introduce myself to myself every morning." I was blown away. She talks to herself? That was unheard of. Or maybe it was simply something that I had not heard. At least my former self had never heard it. That all changed. That very day I wrote my own affirmation and have been quoting it to myself ever since that day.

Now, I know who I am because I keep telling myself who I am. I exist to maximize the potential of individuals and organizations without them feeling alone or overwhelmed about their purpose. This was exactly what I needed to hear. What do you hear? Are you still only hearing the word "no" echo from the hollow and dark cave of your past? How many times have you crash-landed because of the turbulent storms flowing from the cynicism of naysayers, telling you, 'No'? What was the last dream you allowed to go deferred because someone denied you access. Never again. You have the power within to say yes and snatch the hinges off the doors of opportunity that were once closed to you. Why not you? Everyone deserves another chance and you do too. You are allowed to affirm yourself until access is granted, and your future becomes fulfilling. You can say, "Yes." When you speak your "yes" it is enough to depend on. Your personal affirmation is as good a cashed check as Gloria Mayfield Banks', so take it to bank. Decide today to affirm yourself and say, "yes" to your turn.

Live in your now

Today is your day. You cannot go back and change what happened. You cannot unscramble the eggs. What you can do is live today. You are here today and what did not happen before now, you can make happen today. Lao Tzu says, "The journey of a thousand miles begins with one step." You have an opportunity to take your first step today. That step forward will lead you to the jet for your takeoff. It may be scary, and even feel risky. You may second-guess yourself, but, after my experience, I found that what is ahead is so much greater than anything that has already been. Seize this chance to regain what you lost, reclaim who you are, and relaunch a life you were destined for. One of my favorite stanzas is from a poem written by Erin Hanson and reads, "What if I fall? Oh but my darling, what if you fly?" I say to you, make it happen and expect to fly. You have lived the life of pain, rejection, delay and denial. Now live the life you were born to live.

THE COMEBACK

.